Richard Gibbs gained his original degree in Political Science and History at University College Dublin; he converted to law at Birmingham University before reading for the BPTC at the University of Law and then being called to the Bar by The Honourable Society of the Inner Temple where he won the Lawson moot.

He is a practicing barrister prosecuting and defending in regulatory and criminal cases across England & Wales. He has a strong interest in non-CPS prosecutions and has extensive experience of defending individuals and companies in matters relating to Trading Standards and Health and Safety offences. In addition to his practice at the Bar, he is a Visiting Lecturer at the University of Law lecturing aspiring barristers and solicitors in law and the fundamentals of legal practice. He has been a regular contributor to legal journals since becoming a barrister in 2012.

He has appeared on the BBC as a commentator on criminal sentencing and regularly delivers training to police in criminal justice matters. Richard lives with his wife and daughter in Worcestershire.

A Practical Guide to Criminal & Regulatory Proceedings in Consumer Protection Matters

A Practical Guide to Criminal & Regulatory Proceedings in Consumer Protection Matters

Richard Gibbs
Barrister, Inner Temple

Law Brief Publishing

Published 2021 by Law Brief Publishing, an imprint of Law Brief Publishing Ltd
30 The Parks
Minehead
Somerset
TA24 8BT

www.lawbriefpublishing.com

Paperback: 978-1-913715-29-8

For my Mum and Dad and for

Sonya and Freya; my raison d'être

CONTENTS

INTRODUCTION

Categorizing things is something which lawyers do a lot; whether something is criminal or civil; whether it is claimant, prosecution or defendant, private or public law, it is a part of the daily landscape for anyone who practices in the law. That is for many reasons but perhaps it owes part of its explanation to the complexity of the modern legal marketplace and the need – perceived or real – to specialise. Whether that is a good thing or not is an argument for another time and place but it is important when considering issues of regulatory law, both in analysis and its explanation, to bear in mind that those of us who profess to have some understanding of the law, have for many years shaped and molded those categories around us and the work that we do.

Why does that matter? Well, in terms of the items of work and the areas of practice that clearly fall into one of the clearly labeled silos of crime, family, chancery or civil it probably doesn't; perhaps this is the legal equivalent to knowing an elephant when you see one. Whilst acres of text have been expended over the years and many more hours of academic debate and discussion on the topic of what is or is not a crime and what is the distinction between a criminal offence and a civil misdemeanor, it is at the borders between these granular distinctions that real difficulties can arise. That has perhaps always been the case but the pace of that blurring of the lines has arguably quickened in recent years and we have seen a rise in so called regulatory matters; broadly, non-Crown Prosecution Service prosecutions before the Magistrates' and Crown Courts for matters which can entail serious sanctions.

These regulatory offences can be complex and because they exist in the often unclear space between the crime and civil categories of practice, they are often the cause of uncertainty and disquiet, not just among practitioners but also with members of the judiciary. If that were an observation that could just be restricted to one or two small areas of work, then perhaps this would be something too abstruse to be worth expending much energy on. But that is not the case. We are seeing a large number of 'non-CPS prosecutions' come before the courts, from a plethora of alphabet soup named organisations charged with the identification, investigation, enforcement and prosecution of what are very real offences with very real sanctions for the defendant individual, organization or company.

The reasoning behind that is complex but the fact is for the parties who instigated these prosecutions, whether by making a referral or complaint to their local Trading Standards or for the defendants who find they or their company the subject of investigation and prosecution for their behaviour in what often appears to be their commercial dealings, the ramifications and the effects are considerable. Perhaps for too long, the legal profession has viewed this as being outside of the normal scope of many practices simply because the subject matter, at first glance, when viewed through the prism of either a civil or criminal legal approach, appears to be at the margins.

For example, a civil practitioner who is used to dealing with money disputes connected with breach of contract or a failure to perform a specific contractual provision, may view some of the matters which are raised in terms of a prosecution brought by Trading Standards for alleged breaches of the Consumer Protection from Unfair Trading Regulations 2008 or as amended in 2014, as being an unnecessary way of seeking redress for what might appear to be a simple breach of contract. Looked at from that perspective, the most appropriate remedy to what appears to be a breach of contract will be to bring a claim under the Civil Procedure Rules for the remedy of that breach; the aim being presumed to put the claimant in the position they would have been in had the contract been correctly executed or, if rectification is not possible, to recompense them for their loss. Almost certainly, the contract will be examined to explore whether its terms in any way breach the Unfair Contract Terms Act 1977 if the issue applies to businesses, of the Consumer Rights Act 2015 in relation to consumer contracts and notices.

Seen from this angle, notions of prosecuting the breaching party to the contract rather than bringing an action against them for remedy or recovery, may seem both heavy handed and lacking in purpose; the object being presumed to be the recovery of the monies paid or the performance of the task contracted for.

The criminal practitioner on the other hand, would probably look at the problem the other way around but would perhaps agree with the civil practitioners conclusion. For a lawyer used to dealing with a daily diet of criminal fraud, violence, and thefts, references to unfair consumer practices immediately suggests that the matter is one better resolved in the County or High Court rather than the Magistrates' or Crown Court. Again, the presumption is likely to be that the aim of the matter is to recover damages or achieve rectification as opposed to obtaining a conviction.

THE OVERLAP BETWEEN CRIME AND CIVIL

Both views may be right in their narrow confines but both are wrong when it comes to looking at the realities of the law as it presents itself today. We live now in a world of overlapping legal and statutory constructs, each in its own way aimed at rectifying a certain wrong in a certain way but all needing to be looked at holistically and balanced against one another. Thus, the correct answer to a suggestion that a consumer has been treated badly may very well be for one party to be the subject of prosecution for unfair treatment whilst simultaneously consideration is given to civil recovery.

The reasons for that are multilayered but they find some explanation in the revolution in behaviour of consumers over recent years. It is tempting to think that the legal empowerment of consumers comes simply from the actions of the media, from Watchdog through to Rogue Traders and the many websites and consumer forums whose very existence is founded upon the desire to inform and equip wronged consumers of what they can do in order to not simply get redress but more fundamentally, to prevent the same problem recurring.

There are profound and very real arguments regarding the amount and nature of regulation which is imposed upon businesses and trading organisations in England and Wales today and whatever the rights or wrongs of those debates, they are well evidenced and exampled in prosecutions brought under the Consumer Protection from Unfair Trading Regulations ("CPUT"). The casual observer of one of these cases is almost guaranteed to see two diametrically opposed views; from the complainant in the case and from the Trading Standards officers investigating it and bringing the prosecution, there will be a view that such regulations are needed to hold back and limit the behaviour of rogue businesses who through either recklessness or by design, set out to ensure that there are unfairnesses in their dealings which harm the consumer and benefit the trader.

However, to the erstwhile defendant in that situation, they are likely to take the view that whilst modern business and commerce inevitably brings its ups and downs and that whilst problems and mistakes will occur and difficult or problem customers are a fact of life, the red tape and regulatory burden imposed upon businesses and traders – large and small – is such that their hands are tied unfairly when it comes to disputes. To a defendant in such a position, the old maxim that "the customer is always right" may be both wrong in fact and unfairly enforced in law but enforced it is, nonetheless.

TAKING A PRACTICAL APPROACH

The categorization which I mentioned at the start of this introduction, is something which can hinder the practitioner trying to take a practical approach toward the prosecution or defence of such a case. The very unusualness of the cases, fitting neatly into neither criminal or civil practitioners' workload, means that the starting point in case preparation is often further back in terms of knowledge and research than might normally be the case in their work. Further, the practitioner is likely to have to adopt a slightly different approach toward their client than they are perhaps used to; criminal practitioners who prosecute will have become familiar with the policy decisions and cultural mores of the police and CPS but may be less aware of the institutional and systemic attitudes adopted by Trading Standards for example.

Equally, the criminal practitioner who finds themselves defending a client for a CPUT offence before the Magistrates' or Crown Court is likely to find that their client has a very different approach to that adopted by many who find themselves in the dock of a criminal court. For a start they may very well be a company or trading organization symbolized by an individual as opposed to simply a private individual. Secondly, there are likely to be concerns of perception; they are quite likely to feel that they are being unfairly treated. Bringing us back to the conceptual arguments as to whether something should be a civil or criminal matter, the client may well feel that this is something that should be determined either by the parties themselves or between the parties in a civil court without the inherent sense of threat which a criminal court can bring to a defendant. Almost certainly, the process up to that point will have left the defendant feeling 'like a criminal' and this will be something about which they will be aggrieved, whether rightly or wrongly.

THE CIVIL AND CRIMINAL APPROACH

But it is not simply in the management of the case that the criminal practitioner has to amend their approach. They will perhaps be conditioned to think of these cases in terms of the elements of a fraud case. It will not be unusual for a case which has CPUT offences involved in it to also feature frauds; these are matters which often find themselves slotting into both areas and there is a tension as well as a temptation here to retreat into known quantities and familiar territory. As we will see, for the ardent criminal practitioner dealing with a CPUT case, that can cause very real problems.

This book is written from the immediate standpoint of a criminal practitioner who has evolved their practice toward regulatory work but it is as true to say that the civil practitioner operating in this field needs to take stock of their working practices and approach as for the criminal practitioner. Civil lawyers are likely to find themselves on the end of enquiries for advice or representing corporate entities and traders in these matters quite simply because they are more likely to be already in contact with such a putative client. A firm of commercial solicitors or a barrister undertaking general chancery work, may well find that a client with whom they have had some dealings – perhaps through the formation of a company or as a result of entreaties for advice on contract formation – approaches them first and foremost when Trading Standards make known that they are interested in exploring a facet of their trading or when what seemed to be a simple matter of customer dissatisfaction has elevated into an interview under caution.

As much as the criminal practitioner may find themselves out of their comfort zone dealing with a matter whose substance appears to be based more in the realms of the White Book than Archbold, their civil colleague is as likely to feel discomforted by the criminal procedure and process deployed in a Trading Standards investigation and the fact that the outcome will be in a very different form to that which they are more familiar with.

Of course, there are many practitioners who are in the truest sense, generalists; those for whom a diet of varying tribunals and rules of evidence are a staple and not an anomaly. For them, the task of taking on board matters of civil and criminal legislation and procedure and rules of criminal evidence will be second nature. The reality however is that such beasts are rare. Certainly there are members of the legal profession who can switch and turn from one area of discipline and practice to another with ease and flair but for most of us, the need to specialise within our categories and sub sets means that the arrival of a case which is founded on alleged breaches of the Consumer Protection Act or the CPUT regulations will mark a departure from the normal diet to which our constitutions have become accustomed.

The aim of this book is to provide a practical guide to all practitioners dealing with the Consumer Protection Act and the CPUT regulations that came before them. The legislation is complex in its formation and whilst there is a narrative that runs through it, the course of its development is not always clear and predictable. For anyone surveying a construct, it helps to know a little about how it came into being; who built it, when, how and why and this is the approach I take in looking at the legislation as it is currently drafted.

The Consumer Rights Act 2015 has sought to coalesce the issues faced in disputes between consumers and traders into a single place and it is a helpful piece of legislation in that sense. However, partly because of the length of time which passes between alleged offences, their investigation and the litigation process, there are many cases which will still be framed by the terms of earlier legislation and to that end I have sought to give something of an overview of the architecture which is in place.

I have done that not in order to simply give an academic overview but to map out the network of legislation under which these types of Trading Standards instigated cases fall into. There is a clear sense that consumer focused legislation is developing in a certain direction and it is likely that we will see, in the coming years, a greater emphasis on the bringing of prosecutions against all manner of firms and trading entities who are said to have acted unfairly or in such a way as to have harmed a consumer.

This book was first considered before the onset of the Covid-19 pandemic. As far as the effects of that pandemic are concerned, the kaleidoscope has been shaken and the pieces are still in flux; for businesses, traders, consumers, lawyers and the courts. What will happen to many businesses remains to be seen but what can be said almost without fear of contradiction, is that the acute threat posed by truly rogue traders to the consumer will if anything increase as the UK economy moves through and emerges from the pandemic.

Equally, to a trader accused of acting unfairly – and I use that term generically –the impact of the accusation, investigation and perhaps a conviction, is likely to be even more acute than in previous times. Not only are we in an age where negative commercial publicity can be circulated and published with even greater damaging effect than any time in the past but with tightening margins and a very real existential threat to practically every business in the land, allegations of impropriety toward consumers really could be the death knell for any accused trader.

With all and any rights come duties; the more that the first is increased, the more the later must go up too. It appears to be a settled direction of travel that consumer rights are not only here to stay but that they should grow to take account of the increasing ambit of consumerism and its operation, online as well as in the real world. Coupled with our ever more litigious culture, there is an irresistible sense that traders and consumers will continue to form an important cohort of litigants before the courts. As long as that continues to be the case, it is important that practitioners wanting to play a part in providing professional advice and representation understand the legislation under which they are operating and the practicalities of approaching such cases. That is the case in all situations but in an area such as this where the parameters of practice overlap between disciplines and ways of working, it is perhaps even more vital.

Many of the observations and analysis in the pages that follow are ones with which other practitioners may take a different view. They are not stated here to form a corpus of work which can be presented as the definitive work on this subject simply because such a task is impossible. Every case will be different and the approach every practitioner takes will, by necessity, be different. The thoughts and observations which are presented here are meant to be a useful starting point for a practitioner coming to this area rather than a set of rules that should or could be followed to reach a certain outcome.

In every sense this book is intended to be a practical guide to a practitioner in this area and the hope and intention is that these pages will give a useful overview and starting point to the many lawyers now finding themselves defending and prosecuting matters linked to consumer affairs before the courts but whose professional experience may sit slightly askance the subject matter at hand.

The contemporary lawyer knows that the law evolves and changes at a blistering pace and the evolution of new ways of buying and selling goods and services for both businesses and individuals will mean that the tempo is only likely to increase. Nothing can be said with confidence about that but what can be said is that the law as stated in the pages that follow is correct in its application to England and Wales as of 1st January 2021.

Richard Gibbs
Barrister
January 2021

PART ONE

THE LAW AND ITS DEVELOPMENT

Like many areas of legislation, the law as it currently stands in relation to consumer protection and unfair contracts generally, derives from many previous individual strands. Undoubtedly the starting points are varied but it is important to be aware that the earliest legislation in this area – the antecedents of the current legislative framework – started out with very different aims to the contemporary legislation. Partly, this is because consumers and the transactions that they performed were less complex but so was the corresponding scope of those that we would now call rogue traders to exploit and harm consumers in the marketplace.

The nature of the marketplace itself has altered as well. It is no longer purely a location in which trading occurs. It is now as much a process comprised of varying types of transaction, some performed automatically, some through standard forms of agreement and arrangement and others through direct engagement between purchaser and seller in a way that is more traditional but perhaps through different mediums. It is now commonplace for an individual to be involved in transactions which cross borders and which feature a multitude of different organisations as intermediaries for payments, deliveries, orders and advertising.

A trader based in a small market town in England can now market their goods or services in a global marketplace as easily as they could have done so in their town square a generation ago. Through relatively cheap and simple means, the internet can be used by a sole trader to form not just a shop window for their wares but also a vehicle for the receipt of payments directly to their bank, taken directly from the bank of the purchaser – or from a credit providing intermediary – all of which can be concluded after the presentation, offer and acceptance of a contract is carried out. The trading power of what is in reality a business encapsulated within one individual or perhaps a small group of people is now akin to the trading strength and reach of the great trading conglomerates and empires of a previous age.

So as the world has become more complex, so have our patterns of commercial and economic activity and with that growth in complexity the legislative coverage, providing rights to consumers balanced by commensurate duties upon traders, has grown. But this is not the only reason for that spawning of legislation over the last century or so. Added to the changed architecture of our buying and selling patterns however has been a cultural shift which has also informed the formation of legislation in this area.

It is a truism that legislation in England and Wales is as likely to be derived from the international stage, most notably the European Union, but this is not the only cultural informant of legislative development. Whereas the phrase *caveat emptor* would once have been considered the overriding imperative in relations between buyer and seller, between trader and consumer, there is now perhaps a prevailing view that the power balance between the two sides of the coin is not a fair one and so the pendulum should swing toward the perceived smaller actor in the situation, the consumer.

CHAPTER ONE

EUROPEAN UNFAIR COMMERCIAL PRACTICE DIRECTIVE 2005/29/EC

Though by no means the first relevant piece of legislation in time, a useful starting point in the consideration of the legislative evolution in this area is the EU directive on unfair commercial practices from 2005. The Directive was the culmination of longstanding concerns that there was a need on a pan European basis to boost the confidence of consumers whilst simultaneously making it easier for businesses to trade on a cross border basis. The emphasis was particularly upon the effects of the EU open market upon small and medium sized businesses together with their ability to trade across borders.

The intention behind this and other EU directives which address unfair commercial practices is best summed up by considering them as an attempt to enable a panoply of national enforcement agencies to limit a very wide range of unfair business and trading practices. Whilst it is right to say that different countries have differing problems in terms of these issues, a series of common points were identified as crossing national boundaries; the provision of untruthful information to consumers and aggressive marketing techniques designed to influence the choices of consumers.

DIRECTIVE (EU) 2019/2161 AND THE NEW DEAL FOR CONSUMERS

The original directive from 2005 was transposed into national laws by the member states and in England and Wales became the Consumer Protection from Unfair Trading Regulations 2008, a piece of legislation with which the putative practitioner in this area will need to become familiar with. However, in terms of the evolution toward CPUT, the 2019 directive came into being on 27th November 2019 addressing better enforcement procedures and a general modernization of the EU's consumer protection rules. This was all encompassed in what became the EU's New Deal for Consumers initiative.[1]

So as to properly understand the way that the legislation has evolved, it is worth digressing briefly to look at this because it explains the fundamental policy approach adopted by the EU which has gone on to inform the formation of domestic legislation in this area.

This initiative was unashamedly aimed at strengthening the enforcement procedures of the bodies tasked with the monitoring and enforcement of consumer law across the EU. There was consensus that the risk of EU wide infringements was a growing one and that in order to combat this it was necessary to modernize the pre-existing EU consumer protection rules. To that end, the Commission adopted this initiative on 11th April 2018.[2] In the communication which was issued by the European Commission to the European Parliament, the Commission tellingly begun by stating that the aim was to "build a fair Single Market for consumers and businesses."[3] It is clear from the text of that document that the Commission prided itself on the argument that the EU had the strictest rules on consumer protection in the world at that point and deemed that the rights which had been put in place for consumers at that time gave both predictability and confidence to consumers in their dealings with businesses.

Expressly, the Commission acknowledge that the new and evolving marketplace brought about new challenges and that these challenges required an enhancement of enforcement policies and structures. There can be no doubting upon reading that Communication that the EC

---

[1] https://ec.europa.eu/info/law/law-topic/consumers/review-eu-consumer-law-new-deal-consumers_en

[2] This took the form of two proposals for Directive and a Communication, COM(2018) 183 and COM(2018) 184. The proposed amendment to Directive 2009/22/EC came in COM (2018) 185

[3] https://eur-lex.europa.eu/legal-content/EN/TXT/?qid=1573718927782&uri=CELEX%3A52018DC0183

gave a centrality to the interests of consumers, perceived or otherwise, in its initiatives.[4] The document goes on to signpost negotiations taking place then between the European Parliament, the Council and the Commission in relation to digital contracts proposals which was a central element of the Digital Single Market strategy which aimed to modernize consumer contract rules for the supply of digital content and the for the sale of goods. It stated in clear term that the proposals were so important to the ensuring consumers were provided with a clear and effective rights when accessing digital content and ensuring that both consumers and businesses could rely upon uniform and effective rules, that it was necessary for the measures to be adopted rapidly and on a cross border basis.

Self-congratulatory in tone though aspects of the Communication were – and perhaps at odds with the then experience of many seeking redress before national courts for allegations of alleged or real consumer protection issues – the EU recognized that there were very real policy challenges before it at that time. There had been large scale abusive practices such as 'Dieselgate; in which car manufacturers had installed technology in cars to apparently cheat emissions tests and the widespread use by banks of unfair contract terms in mortgage contracts.[5]

Broadly, the New Deal for Consumers legislative proposals encompassed five directives; the Unfair Commercial Practices Directive, the Unfair Contract Terms Directive, the Injunctions Directive, the Consumer Rights Directive and the Price Indication Directive.

---

[4] These took the form at that time of the Digital Single Market strategy which brought about legislation to end mobile phone and data roaming charges, a ban of geoblocking of internet content which prevented consumer access to products and services from a website based in another Member State and cross border portability of online content services from 1st April 2018.

[5] The second issue here in relation to mortgages was addressed by Directive 2014/17/EU on credit agreements for consumers relating to immovable property and this amended Directives 2008/48/EC and 2013/36/EU. Regulation (EU) No 1093/2010 is applicable to mortgage contracts concluded as from 21st March 2016. Amongst other things this requires lenders to provide clear and detailed information on loan conditions to consumers and it provides the consumer with the right to repay credit and an earlier point than was determined by the contract.

As we have already seen, the Unfair Commercial Practices Directive from 2005 aimed to boost consumer confidence and ease the making of cross border transactions and trade but equally providing for the enforcement of rules to curb a broad range of unfair practices. That Directive was amended following presentation by the Commission in May 2016 of an updated version of the 2009 Guidance document.

THE UNFAIR CONTRACT TERMS DIRECTIVE [6]

This directive is aimed at the protection of consumers in situations where unfair standard contract terms are imposed upon them by traders. It applied to all kinds of contacts in relation to the purchase of goods and services and has an application to online as well as off-line purchases of consumer goods and financial services. Loans are covered by this directive. As will by now be apparent, in line with the lifespan of practically all European Directives and the initiatives which underpin them, this directive has undergone amendment. In this case it has been amended by Directive (EU) 2019/2161 on 27th November 2019 which, once again addresses the better enforcement and modernization of the consumer protection rules hitherto in operation across the EU as part of the New Deal for Consumers.

Importantly, the obligation for Member states to provide for effective penalties for infringements is stipulated in the amendment, it was not in its predecessor. The current timeframes for the transposing of this provision into national law is 28 November 2021 and it must be applied from 28th May 2022.

Standard contract terms within the purview of this directive are those which facilitate commercial transactions and it is argued that they can be useful in the setting down of rights and commensurate obligations of the parties involved in the formulation of a given contract. Expressly, the commentary to the directive makes reference in relation to standard contract terms to the notion that the seller and suppliers in any such arrangement enjoy a considerable advantage over consumers by defining

---

6 93/13/EEC

contractual terms in advance and of course without individual negotiation.[7]

There is a stipulation that standard contractual terms must be drafted in language deemed to be plain and intelligible with ambiguities within the language to be interpreted in favour of the consumer. Any terms which are unfair are deemed not to be binding upon consumers and this is rooted in the argument that if the terms are contrary to the requirements of good faith, causative of a significant imbalance in the parties' rights and obligations which are to the detriment of the consumer, that must be axiomatically the right manner of interpretation.

It is not difficult to see how there could be myriad examples of terms which are outside of the ambit of fairness and balance but the Annex to the Directive attempts to provide a non-definitive list of such example terms.

In relation to European founded legislation, this stage perhaps provides a stepping off point to the framing of English legislation in this area. It is important to note that as we depart the European Union, many of the central aspects of the European legislation in this are already implemented within English law and for all practical purposes, as the UK departs from the European Union – with or without an agreement on trade – it is hard so see how there will be much divergence from either the principle or the realities of legislation in this area.

What may change is the evolution of domestic legislation but whilst that is conjecture for the future, the established direction of travel on consumer related legislation is somewhat entrenched now and it is hard to see how there could or would be much by way of substantial departure from that. Irrelevant of that, whatever the future holds, we can see that the development of the European Directives lead to the foundation of the English law which we will now move on to chart.

---

[7] See the discourse on the website of the European Commission about this issue at https://ec.europa.eu/info/law/law-topic/consumers/consumer-contract-law/unfair-contract-terms-directive_en

CHAPTER TWO

PRODUCT LIABILITY DIRECTIVE AND CONSUMER PROTECTION ACT 1987

The Consumer Protection Act 1987 was the implementing legislation in the UK for the European Directive on product liability.[8] Fundamentally, from the perspective of the practitioner, this is the piece of legislation which introduced a clear measure of strict liability into the arena of product liability.

Section 2(1) of the Consumer Protection Act 1987 (CPA) introduces the concept of strict liability where a defective product has caused damage. In essence, this provision provides that where any damage is caused, wholly or in part, by a defect in a product the producer of that item and a variety of others shall be liable for the damage.

DEFINITIONS

In order to dismantle that concept, it is important to firstly understand what a product is. Section 1(2) gives the first part of this interpretation as being "...any goods, or electricity and...includes a product which is comprised in another product, whether by virtue of being a component part or raw material or otherwise." There is no escaping the breadth of that definition and the construction of the definition gives rise to the inescapable conclusion that it was always intended to have a particular wide definition. Again, it might be possible to interpret this piece of statutory instruction as being to give as strong a tilt as possible toward the rights of consumers and the commensurate responsibilities and obligations upon traders. From the start, this casts the net of strict liability wide.

---

[8] This was a European Council directive on the approximation of the laws, regulations and administrative provisions of the Member States concerning liability for defective products, Dir. 85/374; O.J. 1985 L210/29

However, that is not the end of the definition because further points are to be found within s.45(1) CPA. Whilst s.45(1) specifies the interpretations to be given to various terms within the act, an important point here is that the definition is wider than that found in the Sale of Goods Act 1979 because here, goods which are attached to land are included whereas under s.61(1) of the Sale of Goods Act 1979, goods had to be severed before or under the contract of the sale.

That breadth of definition has, since 2000 included liability for damage caused by agricultural and fishery produce.[9] Reflecting the wide nature of this point of definition, the courts determined that transfused blood was a good for the purpose of the act in *A v National Blood Authority.*[10] However the picture is less clear when one comes to look at products such as software or intellectual goods and there is considerable debate around whether the definition in the CPA stretches far enough to encompass such items.[11] One is tempted at this point to suggest that the inexorable direction of travel of the law in this area tends towards an ever greater expansion of such definitions and so it is perhaps more likely than not that the courts will encompass these less tangible products into the definition as time goes by. It is clear to see how wide ranging would be the ramifications and how potentially wide-reaching would be potential litigation in such circumstances but for now it appears that debate continues.

Section 3(1) of the CPA gives definition to the key question of when a product is considered to be defective. Almost inevitably, cases in this area have as part of their make up a conflict of evidence as to whether a product is or is not defective. The CPA definition here is that a product is defective if "...the safety of the product is not such as persons generally are entitled to expect...in the context of risks of damage to property as well as in the context of risks of death and personal injury."

---

[9] Through SI 2000/2771 which itself reflects a change in the Directive Dir. 99/34: OJ 1999 L141/20.

[10] [2001] 3 All ER 289

[11] For example, see the reference in Butterworths Common Law Series: The Law of Product Liability (2nd Edition) at 4.58 to 4.65

Section 3(2) goes on to provide that the circumstances should be looked at in the broadest, holistic manner. This should include the manner and purpose of marketing, the us of any mark in relation to the product, any warnings or instructions which come with it together with what might reasonably be expected to be done with or in relation to the product.

Perhaps unsurprisingly, this has thrown up a great deal of discussion in the authorities of what circumstances may or may not be relevant. Equally unsurprisingly, the tenor of the authorities here is to point out the need to view each case on its particular merits, so in *Wilkes v DePuy International Ltd*[12] – a case about hip implants – Hickinbottom J drew the conclusion that "in an assessment of whether a product is defective, there is a requirement for the application of judgment to the exercise of balancing all relevant considerations."[13] Which circumstances are relevant and what weight is to be given to both is a matter of the particular facts of any case and as was pointed out in *Wilkes* that assessment may be more difficult in the facts of a particular case than it may appear conceptually.[14]

THE ENTITLEMENT OF THE CONSUMER

The entitlement of the consumer as to what they can expect is a further question, but this is to be resolved by way of an objective test. The relevant question has been held to be what the public's legitimate expectation was, rather than what the public expected.[15] That sounds rather verbose at first glance but the essence of it is what the expectation is legitimate although it should be noted that in *Wilkes* Hickinbottom J described Burton J's use of the phrase "legitimate expectation" as "an unnecessary and unhelpful gloss" on the CPA.[16] It is within the generality of comments made in those paragraphs that Hickinbottom J con-

[12] [2016] EWHC 3096 (QB), [2017] 3 All ER 589

[13] Ibid at 78

[14] See para 79

[15] Per Burton J in A v National Blood Authority [2001] 3 All ER 289

[16] See para 71 *Wilkes*

cluded that the test was an objective one and that the level of safety is not one to be assessed by a reference to any actual expectations of a definable group of individuals. It is therefore an objective test in the true sense of the term rather than something to be benchmarked against a set of given expectations or defined expectations from a particular group.

The seminal point here of course is that the consideration will be different in each case and it will be necessary to look at the factors influencing each case separately in order to properly conclude whether or not there was a legitimate expectation. If that complexity were not enough, it is likely that these considerations will be going on in parallel to others in such a set of litigation as for example, the producer of an allegedly faulty good may find themselves being the subject of proceedings under the CPA whilst also being prosecuted for offences under other pieces of legislation; all of that litigation arising out of the same alleged fault in the same item which has caused damage in some way.

INHERENTLY UNSAFE PRODUCTS

Of course, not all products are safe per se and there are many items which have as an inevitable and sometimes even intended consequence of their operation, a degree of risk and an inherently unsafe nature. In cases relating to such products, the fact that there is an inherently unsafe characteristic does not mean automatically that the product is defective. Take for example a cup holding extremely hot coffee. The coffee would always have been intended to be extremely hot, that is in its nature and it is accepted that whilst the product is hot to enhance the consumers enjoyment of it, that heat can equally be dangerous or harmful.

In a case involving extremely hot coffee placed into substantial polystyrene cups, it was not considered that a product was defective despite the inherent danger of the hot coffee.[17] The linked concepts of risk/benefit and the possibility of harm being avoided, must be weighed and balanced. In order for the inherently unsafe product to be deemed defec-

[17] B (A Child) v McDonalds Restaurants Ltd [2002] EWHC 490 (QB)

tive, there must be something more than simply the fact of the item being unsafe. This is the essence of the risk/benefit analysis point.

In *Wilkes* that very issue was central to the judgment of Hickinbottom J and he took as his starting point the issue in relation to medical products. Such items, if effective, can never be entirely safe; the act of invasive surgery coupled with the implant of something which is fundamentally a foreign body as far as human tissue is concerned, is something which can never be devoid of risk. It is inherently unsafe.

The concept of safety is therefore a relative one and that the important point here is that the potential benefit of the item – in that case hip replacements – has to be balanced against the risks of its deployment. That relative concept of safety of course includes the potential utility of the item concerned. Taking the analysis a step further, Hickinbottom J opined that the "practicability of producing a product of risk-benefit equivalence must therefore potentially be a relevant circumstance in the assessment of a products safety."[18]

But that approach relates to a positive scenario; in *Wilkes* the discussion at hand was about the risk/benefit of implanting a replacement hip joint and the varying considerations, including costs, which had to be borne in mind in that procedure and the planning for it. In that situation and others like it, there is a tacit acceptance of risk because the item is inherently something which imports to the consumer not just the benefits from its utility but also, unfortunately, the increased risk to the person in whom the implant is inserted.

The other side of the coin are situations where that risk is not one which is positively recognized and taken on in the manner of a patient. In *B v McDonalds* the question of 'avoidability' was addressed head on and it was concluded that in an appropriate case, the ease and the extent to which a risk can be either eliminated or mitigated, may be a circumstance that bears upon the issue of the level of safety that the public generally is entitled to expect. Whilst this consideration will never be determinative, it is important because there will be as many cases in this arena that arise as a consequence of the handling of an item as apparent-

[18] See para 82 of Wilkes

ly innocuous as a coffee cup as there will be from the surgical implanting of relatively complex and sophisticated items such as hip replacements.

In both, a degree of risk/benefit analysis comes to the fore but the question of 'avoidability' and the lengths to which mitigation can arise from that are in truth questions of the degree to which harm could have been averted, are important considerations in any litigation in this field.

STANDARD v NON-STANDARD PRODUCTS

The CPA is heavy on definitions as mentioned earlier but the authorities which have sprung up in consequence of the litigation flowing from it have had to delve further into interpretation matters and so it is unlikely in the extreme that the practitioner finding themselves perusing the terms of the CPA in a case, will be able to avoid references to authorities on these points of interpretation and construction. Even a cursory investigation into the pertinent authorities will show that the dicta of Burton J and Hickinbottom J in the cases of *Wilks* and *A v NBA*, yield the lions share of relevant and helpful descriptions.

Burton J used *A v NBA* to set out a division among defective products and not just between products deemed defective and those which may not be. He set down firstly 'standard' product which are those which perform as the producer of the product had intended and on the other side of the divide 'non-standard' products. These are products which are different to other products of the same type or model because of something which marks that batch or group out as different, perhaps an error in the manufacturing process.

With regard to 'non-standard' products, the seminal question that should be asked is whether the harmful characteristic was one that was socially acceptable. The case he was deciding was in relation to blood, specifically blood which was contaminated. At the risk of repetition, each case must be assessed on its widest facts and as holistically as possible and the practitioner entering into this field will be aware that cases which address questions such as the social acceptability of contaminants in blood may not always find direct parallels with an assessment of relevant factors in many other areas.

In fact in *Wilkes* Hickinbottom J made clear that he considered that approach to be "positively unhelpful and potentially dangerous" as well as being "unnecessary and unhelpful." Aside from questions as to how likely it ever was that Burton J's distinction would survive, the practitioner is perhaps best directed here to firstly the general narrative which appears in the authorities because this casts light on the factors which are often important in any general cases assessment but perhaps more directly, it is far more likely that a successful claim can be brought in this area where a particular product fails to meet its own specifications.

That avoids the need for the sort of intellectual complexities which Burton J's approach gave rise to and whilst they may be academically of interest, the reality is that a clearer line can be found in terms of judging a product by its own standards. Evidentially this is likely to be a more straightforward exercise and it is probable that the answer – if there is something so clear cut – to the case, will be found in the product's own description of its utility or purpose. There are of course other indicators of liability, potential as well as actual.

REGULATORY OR STANDARDS COMPLIANCE

If a product has been produced without compliance with any relevant mandatory standard which have an application to that product, that will provide prima facie evidence of defect. However, this should be seen as a starting point and in and of itself this may not be enough to found liability.[19]

In *Wilkes,* Hickinbottom J suggested that compliance with the pertinent standards will provide evidence that, in terms of the matters to which those standards are directed, the level of inherent safety required by the CPA has been satisfied. The follow-on conclusion is that in this sense, the product is not therefore defective. So, this is perhaps both a matter of principle and evidence because looking at what Hickinbottom

[19] Pollard v Tesco Stores Ltd [2006] All ER (D) 186 (Apr,) CA

J went on to say; "...in an appropriate case, compliance with such standards will have considerable weight; because they have been set at a level which the appropriate regulatory authority has determined is appropriate for safety purposes."[20]

As a starting point therefore, regulatory compliance can be seen as supportive of a determination that a product is safe but only insofar as that regulatory regime is concerned and only within the limits of what that compliance means for the product. In *Pollard* a child swallowed dishwasher powder having been able to open a supposedly child resistant lid. That lid was found not to comply with British safety standards but nonetheless the court did not find the item to be defective. Instead in that case Laws LJ placed an emphasis on the expectations of consumers as opposed to a legal test requiring the court to look at the safety that such persons would generally be entitled to expect.

What of course has to be kept in mind is that the simple fact of regulatory approval is not axiomatically indicative of there being a defence under the CPA; such approval by a regulator may be powerful evidence that the level of safety of the product was that which people generally were entitled to expect, but there is no automaticity to that conclusion and the practitioner should be wary of concluding that regulatory compliance is a golden bullet in a case. It is a powerful piece of evidence, an excellent starting point, but it is not the end of the matter.[21]

WRONGFUL USE OF A PRODUCT

The misuse of a product is a major cause of problems and it is frequently the case that a defendant producer in this area will pray in aide the fact that the product they have developed has been misused in some way. It is quite feasible that a product is perfectly safe but it becomes unsafe if misused; it is not hard to think of a multitude of household items which satisfy that definition.

---

[20] At paragraph 97 of Pollard

[21] At paragraph 101 of Wilkes

An important question to ask in this scenario is whether the misuse was foreseeable and if it was, whether it was likely that such misuse would have harmful consequences. In such circumstances, it is possible that a warning or cautionary note should have been provided with the product but it is also possible that it should perhaps have been produced in such a fashion that such misuse would have been prevented or at the very least, that the risk of this should have been reduced.

Various examples may be considered here; for example, if a household appliance could generate enough heat through its operation to potentially ignite combustible soft furnishings, one may expect there to be a warning with the product making plain that it should not be left on furniture or anything which could combust. Barbecues frequently come with warnings about the manner in which gas bottles are attached and detached and that there is a risk of explosion if they are not handled in accordance with certain procedures.

Once more, each case has to be looked at on its own merits but simply because an item has caused damage or harm, does not mean that it is defective. The manner of its operation or use must be looked at and even then, it has to be carefully considered whether that is something that should have been the subject of a forewarning from the manufacturer. This does not have to reach to extreme limits but there should be at least a consideration of this.

POTENTIAL DEFECTS

It is self-evident that some potential defects are more impactful than others. The safety requirements which consumers are entitled to expect will vary depending on the specific products being considered and their usage. For example in *Boston Scientific Medizintechnik GmbH v AOK Sachesen-Anhalt*[22]consideration was given to a pacemaker and an implantable defibrillator. Because of the specific products in this case, and the extremely vulnerable situation of patients who were the consumers of these devices, it was perhaps unsurprising that the court held that the safety requirements which these particular consumers were entitled to

22 C-503/13 and C504/13

expect were of a particularly high level. It goes without saying that inherently, if the items malfunctioned there was a considerable potential for damage.

The issue of batches or groups of products was examined in this case and the court formed the view that where it was found that products belonging to the same batch or part of the same production run had a potential defect, it was possible to classify all others in that batch or production run as defective. This is important as it means that there is no requirement to show that the specific product in question is defective, just that it is part of that wider defective category.

It is difficult to think of how a product such as a pacemaker could be used without absolute confidence in it and even the identification of a defect in such a product could only be carried out by reversing a process of complex and invasive surgical procedure so it is understandable that the court took the approach it did to the question of proof defect in a specific product. Once more, that is not to say that the exact same approach will be taken in relation to all product defect issues and it remains to be seen how the courts will approach these questions in different cases, but it is likely that they will have at least a passing acquaintance with the consequences of defect and the steps needed to establish that there is such a defect.

PROVING PRODUCT DEFECTS

The burden of proof in establishing that a product was defective rests with a claimant asserting it though there is no need for a judge to ascertain the precise cause of that defect.[23] In some senses however, this may be an academic point as whilst the CPA does not require the precise cause of the defect to be established, in order for causation to be proven, it is highly likely that the precise cause of the relevant defect will require examination.

The claimant bares the burden of proof but must also evidence not simply that there is a defect but also that this defect caused the perti-

[23] *Ide v ATB Sales Ltd* [2008] EWCA Civ 424

nent loss. The stream of logic here is straightforward and clear but in practice this often proves far more difficult than envisaged. It may, for example, be necessary to identify a very precise defect in order to demonstrate that it has a causal link.

Where a defect in an item is alleged to have increased the risk of harm, the question as to what precisely a claimant must prove becomes a vexed one. There is authority that the claimant is required to prove that the risk of the adverse event suffered had doubled, a high threshold indeed. This was in relation to a case involving the use of oral contraceptives but as has already been seen in the authorities in relation to the CPA, the principles expounded in cases of sensitive, medicinal type products, often see an application far wider than that.[24]

Looking at the situation objectively, it is hard to see how the erstwhile practitioner can be expected realistically to advance many cases with the expectation of showing that the risk of the adversity had doubled. It appears that the Supreme Court agrees, albeit tentatively as in the case of *Sienkiewicz v Greif*[25]very different views were taken as to the appropriateness of the doubling test and whether further evidence is necessary. Although those observations were ventured obiter, it is important to note that divergence of judicial commentary on the appropriateness of such a test.

It seems that a viable alternative could be to say that the court, once satisfied that the level of safety was below that which it should have been, should then go on to find that causation has been proven on the basis of a material contribution. Just this approach was left open by *Wilkes*[26]and there is pre-existing authority in the shape of *Fairchild v Glenhaven Funeral Services Limited.*[27]

Reverting for a moment to the European sphere which gave birth to the CPA, the CJEU has concluded that it is a matter for national courts to

---

[24] XYZ v Schering Health Centre Limited [2002] EWHC 1420 (QB)

[25] [2011] UKSC 10

[26] At para.137

[27] [2002] UKHL 22

decide what evidential rules to apply, the only rider being that this must be done in such a way so as not to displace the burden of proof under the Directive. Equally the effectiveness of the liability system established by the Directive should not be displaced but other than that, the member states are left to their own devices to settle such questions.[28]

WHO HAS A RIGHT OF ACTION UNDER THE CPA?

Locus is established in terms of the CPA by a claimant being able to demonstrate that they have suffered damage of a kind which is addressed by the CPA. S.5 of the Act restricts damage to personal injury or death, or to any loss or damage to property which is for private occupation, use or consumption.[29]

It is permissible for a non-consumer of a product to bring a claim for personal injury or death but claims for damage to property can only properly be brought by consumers. Loss which is of a purely economic form is not covered by the CPA.

[28] See *W v Sanofi Pasteur* (C-621/15)

[29] See Sections 5(1) and 5(3) CPA.

CHAPTER THREE

THE CONSUMER CONTRACTS (INFORMATION, CANCELLATION AND ADDITIONAL CHARGES) REGULATIONS 2013

The Consumer Contracts Regulations (CCR's) are applicable to contracts made both on business premises but also away from them and so apply to contracts made at one remove. These regulations affect large numbers of businesses which contract with consumers and that is irrespective of the location and manner by which the contract is entered into. Where they do not apply are in circumstances were traders buy goods or services from a consumer; equally, they do not apply to contracts formed between consumers on a peer-to-peer basis.

They require detailed information to be provided to consumers and importantly, they make provision for a 14-day cancellation period. There are ancillary prohibitions in the regulations, for example prohibiting the use of premium rate telephone numbers for consumers to use in order to contact a business and there is a prohibition of negative options to sell additional products to consumers that are incidental or secondary to the main contract.

The coverage of these regulations is extremely wide and it is fair to say that they cover most contracts made between consumers and traders but the types of contract are split into three tranches;

OFF PREMISES CONTRACTS

Off premises contracts are sub divided into four further categories. Firstly, a contract which is made where a consumer and trader are together and reach agreement on the contract in a place which is not the traders business premises. This can be at a consumer's home or place of work or almost anywhere else.

Secondly, a contract made where a consumer and trader are together and an offer is made by the consumer in a place that is not the traders business premises. For example, where the consumer signs and order at their home during a visit by a trader and the contract is agreed by the trader at a later date.

Thirdly, a contract which is a greed at a trader's place of business – or through any means of communication immediately after a meeting with a consumer in a place which is not the traders place of business.

An example of this might be where a trader meets a consumer on the street and convinces them that they have a product which the consumer would be interested in buying. They then go to an office or shop which is part of the trader's operation and this is where they sign the contract for the item.

Fourthly, a contract made with the consumer during a trip which is organized by the trader and when it is arranged, the aim of the trader is to sell or promote goods or services to the consumer. There is no definition within the regulations of an 'excursion' but it is feasible that this would cover a scenario in which a trader meets a consumer on holiday and invites them to travel with them to a different venue in order to be sold goods or services.

DISTANCE CONTRACTS

This is where a contract is made between a trader and a consumer where they are not together but where the contract is negotiated and agreed by one or more organized means of distance communication, such as by phone or the internet. The important point to note here is that there must be an *organized* distance selling scheme and the regulations are unlikely to bite in a situation where the selling at a distance is a one off by the trader. A situation where a shop or trader who usually sells items in a direct over the counter type manner provides their goods as a one off through a mail order arrangement to a customer unable to come to the shop is likely to fall outside of the remit of distance contracts under the regulations.

ON-PREMISES CONTRACTS

The regulations provide a set definition here and it is that [an on-premises contract is] "a contract which is neither off-premises nor a distance contract" Effectively, therefore, this means a contract made on business premises, whatever they may be.

It is important to recognise that 'business premises' means a traders permanent premises as well as temporary premises. So if a retailer takes part in a market stall arrangement in addition to their usual retail outlet, that stall is covered by the definition of business premises and it is not possible for the trader to rely upon the fact that these are not their usual or standard business premises.

This is a key definition with regard to these contract types but there is not an exhaustive or prescriptive definition of business premises within the regulations. The practitioner would be well advised when looking at this issue to bear in mind that attempts to proscribe the business premises are likely to be viewed negatively by a court and are likely to be cast relatively widely. That approach is expected both because the alternative would allow traders to benefit from sales from more flexible situations – such as market stalls in addition to fixed retail outlets – whilst at the same time limiting their exposure to the application of the regulations, something which would clearly be unfair.

Equally, as has been seen from earlier discussions of the law in consumer relations more generally, the approach taken is one that priortises the protection of the consumer. Whilst vexatious attempts by consumers should be something that the court targets, a degree of openness is to be expected and preferred in these definitions.

EXEMPTIONS TO THE REGULATIONS

From the above, it can be seen that there are extensive areas of contract which are covered by the regulations and considerable amounts of trading activity will fall within their scope. However, there are some very clear exemptions from them and it is important to note these as providing the limitations for the application of these regulations.

Broadly, nine areas are outside the operation of these regulations;

I. All gambling including partaking in the National Lottery although it should be noted that there is specific legislation which addresses gambling

II. The provision of financial services such as banking, credit provision, insurance and personal pensions. However, both insurance and credit facilities will be affected by the regulations if they are supplied with contracts for either goods or services or when they are offered as part of an optional extra which the consumer must opt out of

III. The construction of new buildings or those which become substantially new through the conversion of existing buildings. The sale of immovable property is also outside of these regulations though they do apply to the construction of extensions to be attached to existing buildings

IV. Residential letting contracts are outside of the scope of the regulations but the contracts with estate or letting agents for their work in connection with the sale or letting of properties are covered

V. The supply of consumable goods by those who make frequent deliveries. The best example of this would be the delivery of milk but the visits to a consumer's home or place of work must be regular and frequent.

VI. Contracts for package holidays are not covered

VII. Timeshare and long-term holidays including both resale and exchange contracts

VIII. Any purchases from vending machines

IX. The provision of single telecom connections, such as pay phones or connections to the internet through internet cafes.

SALES CONTRACTS, SERVICE CONTRACTS AND CONTRACTS FOR DIGITAL SERVICES

The regulations divide and address these three different headings of contract. Firstly, sales contracts include contracts which are made for the sale of goods and services together. Therefore, they would apply to a situation where there was the supply and fitting of a kitchen or bathroom, garden patio etc. Secondly, service contracts; these, as the name implies, are simply for the provision of services alone and do not cover goods. For the most part the provision of household utilities such as gas and water would fall under this heading, though gas bottles would be seen as goods. The professional services of a lawyer or accountant would most certainly be recognized as stand alone services.

The finally of this triumvirate is contracts for digital services and this covers the supply of data in whatever form but through an intangible medium, so streamed films or music are covered.

PROVISION OF INFORMATION

The regulations require the provision of certain information to consumers by traders in relation to goods, services and digital content which is sold from a distance. However these requirements do not apply to all types of contract and there are certain exemptions; for example medical services or products which are either prescribed or dispensed and which are available free under NHS arrangements and contracts for passenger transport services. However it is essential that a trader provide the appropriate information if this contract is concluded by means of an electronic system.

The fundamental requirement is that consumers must be given information in a way which is clear, comprehensible and appropriate to the means of communication and that must be done before the contract is entered into with the trader. Not only must the information be provided eventually away to the consumer, it must also be provided on a medium which is durable. The regulations persist in defining this is being on paper, by email or any other medium allows the information to be addressed personally to the recipient, which enables the recipient to store that information and to access it for future reference-but That includes pleasing information in a customers personal account area of a website so that they can access it by logging in providing their personal details-and which allows and change reproduction that information.

The regulations also outline what is required of the information which trader is required to provide. Firstly, that information must contain the main characteristics of the goods, services or digital content being provided. As much information as the means of communication allowance must be provided.

Secondly, the identity of the trader must be provided. Most importantly this is likely to be the trading name of that trader. In addition to that the geographical address where the train is established together with other such applicable information, such as telephone number, fax number so as to allow consumers to be able to make contact readily and efficiently with the trader.

If there is an intermediary acting on behalf of a trader, for instance a sales organization or website, then the identity of that intermediary organization and their geographical address must also be provided. Again it is not difficult to see why these requirements are in the regulations, but it is equally not difficult to see how in an evermore complex globalized economy and trading environment, the precise geographical location, contact details and even identity of a trader is occasionally a matter of some contention.

Stemming from this, if the trader or intermediary have different addresses for consumer complaints, or simple consumer contact points, then these addresses must be given. This is the case even if it is necessary to provide a number addresses, telephone numbers, and email addresses for example.

Build contact points and addresses, the total price of the goods, services or digital content inclusive of taxes such as VAT must be provided. If the whatever reason this figure cannot be calculated in advance, then the trader is under an obligation to set out how this will be calculated in due course. The key here is that there must be transparency not only of information, but at the methodology for any calculations which will be necessary in order to complete a transaction.

If delivery charges or other ancillary costs are necessary then these must be set out as well. Regulations recognise that it will not always be possible to state in advance precisely what such costs are. However, that does not alleviate the trader of duty to make it plain that there will be such costs. In those scenarios, if these costs cannot be calculated in advance the fact that they will be payable must be communicated in clear terms by the trader to the consumer.

Where a transaction gives rise to an open-ended contract or subscription, the Monthly billing period together with its costs must also be made plain. In addition any costs for using a specific means of distance communication to make the contract, for example if there is a difference between costs for making a purchase by phone as opposed to online, then that must be made clear also. All arrangements for payment, delivery or performance at the time which were taken to the delivery of goods, the performance of services, all the supply of digital content must be set out and made clear as well.

It is clear to see the complaints, their avoidance and their handling, is essential issue in terms of these regulations, as it is or all the regulations which of the subject of this book. Increasingly, traders large and small are being encouraged to have their own complaint handling policy. The practicality of such policies, let alone the contents, is outside of the scope of this book all providers of services should have such a policy in place as required by the Provision of Services Regulations 2009. Additionally, there are various codes of practice and some trade and professional bodies also place requirements upon their members to not only hold a policy, but to make that available to consumers. A wise trader will therefore make sure that at the very least this is signposted to those with whom they do business.

The procedures for exercising rights to cancel, if there is one, should also be included. The regulations themselves provide for Model Instructions for Cancellation and the requisite information under this part of the regulations can be provided by correctly filling in and providing those model instructions for cancellation. In the event that there is an expectation that consumers must pay the costs of returning goods after cancellation, then the trader must tell them. Equally, if the goods cannot normally be returned by post – for example if they are too large – consumers must be advised of the cost of returning. Once more, information may be provided by correctly filling him and providing the model instructions for cancellation.

If there are no cancellation rights or where the trader is aware that there are circumstances in which the consumer will lose their right to cancel, then the trader must inform them of this so as to ensure that the consumer is aware of that possibility from the outset.

If a trader is selling goods, then the consumer should be reminded that the goods which are being sold must be in conformity with the contract. For example, it may be that the trader would want to state that the responsibility to supply goods which meet the consumer's rights, rests with the trader and if there are concerns that those obligations have not been met, then the consumer is able to contact the trader. At first blush this may be seen to be an invitation to complain but the landscape upon which these regulations sit, as do so many, is that of expecting the trader to the initiative and to be proactive in their stance.

The trader should also provide information of any after sales customer service or care that is provided together with the applicable conditions and if the trader is a member of a professional body or where a code of conduct is applicable, then consumers must be told of how they can obtain a copy.

Where a contact is being entered into for a fixed duration, it is imperative that the consumer is informed of what this is and if it has no fixed length but can be extended automatically, then it is important that information is provided which explains under what conditions a consumer can terminate this. if there is a minimum duration under the contact

– often the case for example in the provision of mobile phone services – then that too must feature in the information provided.

If a trader requires a consumer to provide a deposit or any other financial guarantee, then the fact of the obligations together with any additional conditions must be notified as well.

These requirements apply for all types of goods, services or digital content but the digital marketplace has given rise to specific information requirements in this space and the first point of note here is that digital content functionality must feature in the provided information. This includes information about its language, duration, file type, access, updates, tracking, internet connection, geographical or age restrictions and any additional purchases which are required. Allied to that, digital content compatibility information regarding both the hardware and software must be provided.

Finally, information must be provided as to the existence of any alternative dispute resolution schemes which the trader is subject to, as well as information on how to access those schemes. This is as a direct result of the Alternative Dispute Resolution for Consumer Disputes (Competent Authorities and Information) Regulations 2015. This requires those who sell goods and services online to provide certain information regarding ADR Schemes; broadly this should include the provision of a link to the European Online Dispute Resolution platform and an email address for consumers to make contact and additionally, a trader that is committed to using an ADR process must include the ODR link in any emails which it sends to the consumer offering goods or services. This includes reference to the ODR platform in their general terms and conditions for online sales.[30]

[30]https://ec.europa.eu/consumers/odr/main/index.cfm?event=main.home2.show&lng =EN

CONTRACTS CONCLUDED BY ELECTRONIC MEANS

In situations where the contract is concluded by electronic means and an obligation for the consumer to pay is created, the trader must insure that the following are bought to the consumers attention immediately;

- the main characteristics of what is being sold;
- the total price of the goods inclusive of VAT
- all delivery charges or any other costs
- if the consumer will be entering into a fixed term contract, the duration of that arrangement or if it can be extended automatically, the conditions under which they can terminate it
- if there is a minimum duration for the operation of the contract

These must be bought to the attention of the consumer before they place any order. An express acknowledgement from the consumer that they are under an obligation to pay when the order is placed is also needed. Wording such as "order with an obligation to pay" may assist but whatever terminology is used, this should be easily legible and clear in terms of its meaning. If the requirement to communicate this is not met, the corollary of that is that the consumer is not bound by the contract.

CREATING A DISTANCE CONTRACT BY TELEPHONE

The use of telephone calls to conclude distance contracts has perhaps diminished since the internet became the prime means of such transactions, but there are still many cases where transactions are conducted in such a manner. If a telephone call is used to conclude a distance contract, the form of words which is used by the trader is important. They must commence the conversation by providing their identity, or if calling on behalf of another trader, their identity and also the commercial purpose of the call.

After the distance contract has been entered, the consumer must be given confirmation of that on a durable medium. That confirmation must contain the following;

- The main characteristics of the goods, service or digital content;
- The identity of the trader;
- The trader's geographical address
- If the trader is acting on the behalf of another, their identity and address;
- If there is a different address for complaints, that address;
- The total price of the goods, services or digital content inclusive of taxes;
- All delivery charges or other costs
- The monthly or billing period costs of open-ended subscriptions or contracts
- Any additional costs for using a specific means to communicate
- The arrangements for payment, delivery or performance and the time for that delivery or performance
- The complainant handling policy
- Conditions, time limits and procedure for exercising a right to cancel
- If costs are applicable to the consumer for the return of goods following cancellation

- -If there is a service contract then the requirements for costs to be paid by the consumer for services delivered up to the time of cancellation within the cancellation period

- -If there are no cancellation rights, or circumstances in which those rights can be lost, this should be notified to the consumer

- A reminder of the fact that goods sold to the consumer must be in conformity with the contract

- Any applicable terms and conditions which pertain to after sales customer services, assistance or guarantees

- If the traders is a member of a code of conduct, there should be information about how a customer can access this

- if the contract will be of a fixed duration, what that is or the conditions under which it can be terminated if this automatically extends

- If there is a minimum duration of a contract

- If there is a requirement for the giving of a deposit or other financial guarantee together with applicable conditions

- In relation to digital functionality, its language, duration, file type, access, updates, tracking, internet connection, restrictions and additional purchases

- Digital content compatibility

- The existence of any ADR schemes.

This goliath list needs not be provided if it has already been communicated on a durable medium before the conclusion of the contract but the essential point is that it must be provided before the contract is entered into. The latest point at which the information must be given to the consumer is no later than when the goods are delivered. It would therefore be permissible to include these pieces of information within packaging which is attached to the goods.

In relation to service contracts, it should be provided before the performance of the service begins and for digital contend, this should be within a reasonable timeframe. That may mean that it could have been sent by the trader but not received by the consumer before the digital download commences.

RIGHTS TO CANCEL

There is not a right to cancel in every type of contact. In the following cases, there is no right to cancellation;

- medicinal products or services that are either dispensed on prescription or are available free under an NHS arrangement

- a contract for passenger transport services – for example, bus, rail or flight tickets

- the supply of goods or services where prices are dependent upon fluctuations in the financial markets, which are beyond the control of the trader. Utility supplies of water, gas and electricity and district heating are excluded from this exemption (so the right to cancel remains)

- the supply of bespoke goods that are made to the customer's specification or are personalised – for example, a made-to-measure suit or pair of curtains, or a gift that has the recipient's name engraved on it. However, this exemption does not apply to items made to a customer's specification simply by combining stock items – for example, a computer put together from stocked parts or a car ordered from a fixed menu of items

- the supply of goods that are liable to deteriorate or expire rapidly, such as a delivery of fresh flowers or meat

- the supply of alcoholic drinks (such as vintage wines bought for investment purposes) where the following apply:

    - the price has been fixed by the contract

    - delivery can only take place after 30 days

    - the value is subject to market fluctuations beyond the control of the seller

- contracts where the consumer has specifically requested the trader to call to carry out urgent repairs or maintenance. However, this exemption does not apply to other goods or other services provided at the same time. An example would be a plumber who receives a call to replace a broken immersion heater, a price being agreed over the phone, and whilst there also offers to repair a dripping tap; this extra work, if done during the visit, would retain a cancellation right

- the supply of newspapers, periodicals or magazines. However, subscription contracts retain a cancellation right

- contracts concluded at a public auction. However, this exemption does not apply to eBay and other online auctions. Therefore traders selling via so-called online auction sites will have to give consumers a right to cancel and comply with all aspects of these Regulations irrespective of whether they are selling the goods by auction or through 'buy it now' offers. A 'public auction' is defined in the Regulations as "a method of sale where:

    - goods or services are offered by a trader to a consumer through a transparent, competitive bidding procedure run by an auctioneer

    - the consumers attend or are given the possibility to attend in person

    - the successful bidder is bound to purchase the goods or services

- the supply of accommodation, transport of goods, vehicle rental services, catering or services related to leisure activities if the contract provides for a specific date or period of performance – for example, hotel bookings, courier services, car hire, restaurant bookings and theatre tickets for specific dates

Over and above these cases, a consumer will lose their right to cancel in three clearly defined situations; firstly, if they unseal goods which are unsuitable for return if unsealed, due to health or hygiene considerations. Secondly, if they unseal audio, video or computer software that were sealed at the time of delivery and thirdly, if they combine goods with others so that they become inseparable after delivery.

CANCELLATION PERIOD

There are two rights for a consumer who decides they do now with to continue with a contract and those are either to withdraw or cancel the contract. Withdrawal of the offer can take place if the offer has not been accepted by the trader; cancellation can take place under these regulations if it takes place within a specific period of time.

There are different cancellation periods for different types of contract as set out below;

CONTRACT TYPE	CANCELLATION PERIOD
Service contract	14 days, starting the day after the day on which the contract was made
Digital Content Supply (where not supplied on a tangible medium)	14 days, starting the day after the day on which the contract was made
Sales contract for goods or services	14 days, starting the day after the day on which the goods came into the physical possession of the consumer
Sales contract made up of an order for multiple goods delivered on different days	14 days, starting the day after the day on which the last of the goods came into the physical possession of the consumer
Sales contract for regular delivery of goods during a period of longer than one day	14 days, starting the day after the day on which the first of the goods come into the physical possession of the consumer.

CHAPTER FOUR

THE CONSUMER RIGHTS ACT 2015

The Consumer Rights Act 2015 (CRA) is likely to become as ubiquitous in terms of references made to is as a number of the pieces of legislation it replaced, such as the Sale of Goods Act 1979 and the Supply of Goods and Services Act 1982. It came into force on 1st October 2015 and was aimed at making the law in this area both clearer and easier to understand. It addresses itself, as the name suggests, to every business which sells directly to consumers and the raison d'etre behind the legislation was to ensure that there was clarity as to what should happen when goods or digital content is faulty or when the provision of services takes place in such a way as to be without reasonable care and skill.

The legislation is comprehensive in terms of what it defines as well as what it seeks to regulate, and it provides a central tenet of any proper assessment of the legislative landscape. In the CRA we have what amounts to a single set of rules applying to all contracts where goods are supplied by sale, hire-purchase or work contracts as well as where the issue is the supply of services or digital content.

TRADER DEFINED

A trader under the CRA is a person who is acting for the purposes of their business, trade, profession or craft. It can of course mean more than a single individual, so it naturally covers a partnership of two or more people. A person can of course also be a company or charity, a department of government – national or local – or a public authority. If a person, as a trader, allows another to act in their name or on their behalf, they are still responsible for those contracts as a trader.

CONSUMER DEFINED

A consumer is best defined as an individual who in their dealings and interaction with a trader is doing so for the purposes wholly or predominantly outside of their trade, business, craft or profession. Where they are buying goods for personal use but on a trade account, or where they are presenting themselves as a business, the CRA does not consider them to be a consumer. The definition isn't a completely black and white issue; an individual can be considered to be a consumer in some respects when making purchases at a public auction where individual attendance is possible.

It can be envisaged that there are cases where it is in the traders interests to recast the purported consumer as not a consumer as to do so would serve to limit the rights of the purchaser. In those cases, the trader bears the burden of proving that point.

QUALITY OF GOODS

There are certain statutory rights which apply to every transaction under the CRA. Not only must the person making the sale or transfer have the right to do so but the goods must also be of a satisfactory quality. That is judged by them being of a standard which a reasonable person would regard as satisfactory. It is important to remember that in assessing quality, all relevant circumstances must be part of the consideration and that includes price, description and the advertising carried out by the manufacturer. The general term of quality covers a very wide number of matters but it will cover the fitness of the item for the purposes for which goods of that particular kind are normally supplied. Equally the appearance and the quality of the finish of the goods, added to it being free from minor defects will be relevant. Finally, safety and durability will be pertinent.

FIT FOR PURPOSE

Should a consumer make it clear that the goods they are contracting for are required by them for a particular purpose, then the goods should be fit for that specified requirement. This is also the case where it is obvious that the goods are intended for a particular purpose.

Additionally, the goods must match the description of them which was provided. Where a consumer has relied upon a description, sample or a display model, the goods which are then provided must conform to this description. In cases where there is not conformity on this point, it is possible that an offence may have been committed. Should there be a need for installation of the goods. Quality applies to intangible as well as tangible goods of curse and so is as applicable to digital content supplied.

The structure of the CRA is straightforward and is broken down into three specific parts. The first part deals with consumer contracts for goods, digital content and services; part two deals with unfair terms and the final part contains a range of miscellaneous provisions and powers of enforcement.

PART 1

The inclusion of digital content was the most significant and perhaps the most important of the changes heralded by the CRA as previously legislation had focused in exclusively on the more 'traditional' provision of goods and services in their tangible and generic form. Prior to this, intangible digital property did not have the consideration of 'goods' and so whilst music purchased on a CD or tape could be considered as goods, those steamed form the internet could not be. That was because they were not subject to the Sale of Goods Act 1979 but their inclusion by the CRA rectifies that historic omission.

To this end, Part 1 introduces implied terms meaning that digital content must be of a satisfactory quality, fit for a particular purpose and as described to the consumer. If it is not, there is a commensurate right of the consumer to repair, reduction in price or a replacement. Further, there is an entitlement within this part for compensation if digital content supplied causes damage to a consumer's electronic device or other digital content, so long as the consumer is able to demonstrate that the trader failed to exercise reasonable care and skill.[31]

Finally, there is a limited automatic refund right where a consumer has an unqualified right to receive a full refund if the trader has no right to supply that particular digital content.

Part 1 is not exclusive aimed at digital content as it also deals with services. Any service must be performed with reasonable care and skill, it must be undertaken at a reasonable price and carried out within a reasonable time. If these things are not done, then there are remedies of repeat performance or price reduction available to the consumer.

The practitioner assessing a possible case under the CRA should be mindful of the graduated approach; the first step should be for the consumer to seek repeat performance and then to only proceed to step two of price reduction if that is not done in a reasonable time, or if it is impossible. A price reduction can, if appropriate, be for the whole price but any refund must be given without undue delay and at least within 14 days which begins with the day on which the trader agrees that the consumer is entitled to a refund.

PART 2

The focus of Part 2 is unfair contract terms. The effect of the CRA in general and of Part 2 in particular is the merging of the Unfair Contract Terms Act 1977 and the Unfair Terms in Consumer Contracts Regulations 1999. New remedies are now in place for defective or faulty goods and a tiered approach of remedies is set out.

Those are as follows; firstly, short term rejection – within 30 days, although this can be extended by the trader. It cannot be shortened. Secondly, following this, partial rejection or, thirdly, repair or replacement,

[31] Importantly on this point, there need not have been any payment for the digital content and this applies even if it was provided for free.

or, finally, price reduction and a final right to reject. The 30-day period commences on the date upon which all of the following are established;

1) Ownership or possession of the goods has passed to the consumer;
2) The goods were delivered; and
3) If installation or any other action was required to allow the consumer to use the goods, the trader has told the customer that this has taken place.

It is important to emphasise that there is nothing with the CRA which is intended to remove the previous rights of the consumer to seek damages, specific performance, return of the price paid, or repudiation for other reasons.

Before the CRA, the Unfair Contract Terms Act 1977 included a test of fairness in order to assess what was and what was not a fair contractual term. The CRA adopts a uniform test which defines a term in a consumer contract as being unfair if it "causes a significant imbalance in the parties' rights and obligations under the contract to the detriment of the consumer." In assessing whether a term is unfair, the test takes into consideration the circumstances which existed at the time the term was agreed; the other terms of the contract and what is being provided under the contract.

There should be a transparency of terms and they should present as both simple to understand and such as not to take advantage of the vulnerability of a consumer. The legitimate interests of the consumer should also be taken into account.

The fairness test is the subject of exemption and terms which specify the main subject matter or which set the price are not subject to a fairness test if the are plain, intelligible and legible; in other words, if they are transparent. There must also be a prominence to such terms and there is an expectation that they will have been bought to the consumers attention in a way which would mean that the average consumer would know about them.

BLACKLISTED TERMS

The flip side of the exemption is the fact that the CRA contains a number of terms which are automatically deemed to be unfair without any application of the fairness test. If any such blacklisted term appears in a consumer contract, they will therefore be unenforceable. Examples of items which would fall within this category are terms which seek to limit liability for less than the contract price for failure to comply with statutory terms. Terms which seek to exclude liability for failure to perform with reasonable skill and care, those which exclude or limit liability for death or personal injury caused by the trader's negligence are similarly blacklisted and so are not capable of enforcement.

The CRA expressly requires the courts to review contracts for fairness and when there is a dispute – even if the question of fairness has not been raised by the parties – this will be something that the court will review.

Fundamentally, the CRA is a consolidating act, bringing together as it does a number of pieces of legislation and placing them under one roof. There are innovations and clarifications, but it is perhaps best to view the CRA as a consolidating exercise. One of the main reasons that this book sets out several other areas of legislation is that prosecutions and actions are still likely to be bought under legislation other than the CRA, but it would be wrong to ignore such a sizeable and far-reaching piece of legislation.

Through its definitions and through the place it holds as the central piece of English consumer legislations, the argument as to the relationship between consumer and trader can be seen in even starker light. The argument which commenced in Europe, aiming to give the consumer greater weight and a stronger position in their relations with traders, can be argued to have come to English shores most definitely on the giving of Royal ascent to the CRA. Even in the fact that the CRA consolidates other legislation can be sensed the original European desire to give voice to the consumer. No longer, so the argument goes, does a wronged consumer need to wade through myriad regulations and statutory instruments to find the legal underpinning for their grievance. Instead, standing astride the landscape is the CRA 2015, easy to access and written in clear terms.

The practitioner should be aware of this but also should not forget that there are other areas of legislation in which the trader may be found in breach.

CHAPTER FIVE

CONSUMER PROTECTION FROM UNFAIR TRADING REGULATIONS 2008

The Consumer Protection from Unfair Trading Regulations 2008 (CPUT) came into force on 26th May 2008. Echoing their European foundations, the Regulations are intended to protect consumers from unfair or misleading trading practices. They have the effect of banning misleading omissions and sales tactics deemed to be aggressive.

The CPUT Regulations have three distinct sections; a general ban on unfair commercial practices, a ban on misleading and aggressive practices which are assessed in light of the effect that they have, or are likely to have, on the average consumer and finally, the so called 'blacklist' of commercial practices which will always be unfair and so are banned outright.

The practitioner dealing with proposed litigation in this area is likely to come across questions under these sections from the inception of the case they deal with and it is important to understand the methodology of the regulations and the requirements and prohibitions within them. Case preparation really can only begin with a thorough understanding of what may at first blush seem basic points within the CPUT framework. From the beginning, it is vital to recognise that there are real differences between the tests and definitions within the CPUT framework and those which might pertain to other issues in the same case.

For example, it is commonplace for matters to appear on a charge sheet or indictment which address both CPUT matters and fraud; there is a requirement for the evidencing of dishonesty of course in fraud but that need not appear as part of the rubric of a CPUT issue. An offence can be committed under CPUT where there is no dishonesty as the focus instead is on behaviours which can be deemed unfair or otherwise and so a wider assessment of the actions of the trader must be carried out.

Added to that, there needs to be a benchmarking of that behaviour as it appears in the evidence and the behaviour expected – or not allowed – under the CPUT provisions.

MISLEADING ACTIONS

A useful starting point in the analysis of a case in this area is to begin with asking the question as to whether there have been any actions by the trader which can be characterized as misleading. It is an offence under CPUT for a trader to deploy tactics which are misleading or underhand. Of course this a finely balanced question in a number of cases and it is not hard to see how it can be argued that there are many sales techniques and advertising methods which, on some readings, could be seen to be underhand.

However, what we are concerned with here is a misleading action or underhand tactic to get a consumer to part with money or to make a transactional decision which they would not otherwise have made. This is the central point of that part of CPUT; is there something that the trader has done which has compelled the consumer to make an economic decision that they would not otherwise have made? If the answer to that question is a positive one, then there may be a prima facie case to answer and it is here that the practitioner should focus their attention and investigative energies, whether defending or prosecuting.

As an aside, for those prosecuting these cases and receiving papers from Trading Standards at the culmination of an investigation, it is important to understand that assumptions can be made at this point based on a viewing of the case through the prism of witness evidence from a by now aggrieved consumer. Take as an example a kitchen supplier who has contracted to supply and fit a new kitchen at a consumer's home but during the lead up to the physical arrival and installation, relations between the consumer and trader have deteriorated to a point where communications between them are strained and perhaps pointed. In this set of circumstances, it would hardly be surprising if – perhaps based on what can be thought of as a general customer service issue, poor complaint handling for example – a complaint was raised with the relevant Trading Standards team because of what the complainant consumer might very well feel has been unfair practice by the trader.

Trading Standards are bound to then investigate and may be provided with copies of communications that have passed between the consumer and the trader. On reading these, Trading Standards may take a dim view of the wording used or the tone of the trader's communications; perhaps there is a refusal to accept fault or acknowledge where things have gone wrong. It is even possible that a degree of implied threat exists about wanting promised payments to be made in circumstances where the trader perhaps has begun to fear as a result of the deteriorating relationship, they may not be paid the final sum. With all of these points in mind, it would not be difficult to see how a consumer may feel they are being compelled to do something – make payments – that they might not any longer really wish to. The question here though is whether or not they would not have made those payments but for the actions of the trader and that is a far more nuanced question when one is exploring the construction of a case to put before a court than when a Trading Standards officer is making a decision as to whether or not a trader has a case to answer.

It can perhaps be said of all prosecutions that it is wise for the lawyer to step back and examine the issues which underpin the decision to launch an investigation and a prosecution but the purpose of this particular digression is to point out that the labeling is particularly important in CPUT cases. What can appear to be misleading or underhand to a complainant consumer and what satisfies the requirement of those two labels for the purposes of investigation might not axiomatically satisfy the burden which the prosecution has to satisfy in bringing a case before the courts.

Returning to the issue of misleading actions, these can include the advertisement for sale of goods which in actual fact do not exist or even of offering a limited number of items for sale at an advertised price when it is apparent that there is no way of meeting the large demand that such an offer will bring. Comparisons between products are also an area where misleading representations can fall foul of the CPUT regime. Suggesting that a trader's product is twice as strong as a competitor's or will last ten times as long if in fact neither of those things are true, or where the advantage of the one product over the other is less than set out in that representation, would give rise to a breach of CPUT because of the misleading nature of that statement.

It is wise at this point of analysis into a potentially misleading action to look at whether the trader has signed up to a code of practice. There are numerous examples of such codes in being and they are often cited by traders as a hallmark of quality and membership is taken by consumers as a reassurance as to strength and quality of the trader. So at the point at which the actions of the trader are being set against the question of whether their practice amounts to a misleading action, it is worth carrying out a parallel enquiry into any other applicable code of practice because not only could this give rise to a separate issue for the trader in terms of their obligations but from a defence perspective, any tension between what appears prohibited by CPUT and what appears permissible under the industry specific code may give rise to an explanation. It is important to note that this may not give the trader a defence but if it can be correctly identified that they were compliant with an industry specific code, then this may serve to assist the trader when it comes to their efforts to address the case made against them by those acting for the consumer.

So at this point, we can see that misleading actions covers comparisons which are misleading and any tactic which is either misleading or underhand when it is deployed to get the consumer to make a payment or take a transactional decision which they would not otherwise have made. This is not the end of the prohibitions on traders however. They are also banned from providing false information about the characteristics of goods and about whether a product requires servicing or replacement. It can be seen just from that statement that at this point there can be fertile ground for uncertainty between sales pitches and the requirements of the legislation but a granular approach here assists. For example, a trader stating that they only sell genuine branded parts for a machine of some description when the truth is that their stock consists of either non branded parts or perhaps a mixture.

It is not simply the substance of the transaction which is covered by this question, the surrounding rights and duties of the consumer and trader are also pertinent. This arises frequently when questions arise as to the state of knowledge of the consumer about their legal rights and ability to seek redress or a refund, or even to exit the contract or arrangement are concerned. If consumers have been misled about their legal rights, or if the trader has given false or deceptive information about the business or the traders qualifications, that is also something which can be characterized as a misleading action by the trader.

There is much within CPUT which can be seen in a nuanced way and it should be clear from this overview of this one aspect that a misleading action is something that requires real analysis. Simply because the piece of information provided by the trader to the consumer turns out to be wrong, does not automatically render the action of the trader a misleading one. Rather, the circumstances may need to be looked at and the behaviour and actions of the consumer will almost certainly need to be assessed in order to judge what action was and was not a misleading one on the part of the trader.

The question of parallel obligations in terms of the possible membership of a trade specific body also needs to be assessed and it is vital that the practitioner makes themselves aware of the obligations which may be imposed by that organization as well. A failure to abide by such an obligation may lead either to a specific charge or perhaps act to evidence wider CPUT breaches. In either case, purely at the stage of misleading omissions, a holistic and pragmatic approach is required whether defending or prosecuting, to understand that scope of charges which may be pertinent in any given case.

MISLEADING OMISSIONS

It perhaps goes without saying that a consumer can be as mislead by a trader's failure to say or do something as by a positive act on their part. There is of course an overlap here as there may be a deliberate decision not to tell a consumer a certain thing but CPUT places a specific onus on the leaving out of pertinent information.

It may once have been the case that being economical with the truth about something was all part of a trader's approach to marketing their wares or pitching their services, but the wise trader would be well advised now to be aware that such an approach is likely to give rise to allegations that the trader has allowed – or encouraged – misleading omissions in their discourse with the consumer. As all of us know in relation to all manner of scenarios, what is said is not always the problem but rather the issue may well be with what is missed out.

The key question which almost always must be addressed is whether information has been missed out has the effect of preventing the consumer from making an informed decision. The provision of information is as vital in enabling the making of informed and reasoned economic decisions on the part of the consumer as the content of the information communicated. It is not hard to see how an omission could have the effect here of preventing a sensible consumer decision from being effected.

Closely allied to this is the requirement that information be provided in a timely manner. It is no defence to point to the ultimate provision of important information upon which the making of key decisions depends, when there is a time critical element to this. The information must have been provided before the point at which its provision was too late to be of any real use to the consumer.

Therefore we can see that there is a clear onus upon the trader to ensure that they provide information of a sufficient quality and detail and do so in a timely manner. A trader is likely to commit an offence if they act in the following broad ways;

(i) Omitting material information needed by the average consumer in the context of the trade concerned which was necessary for the making of an informed decision by the consumer about the transaction;

(ii) Hiding of information which is material by couching it in a way which is unclear, unintelligible, ambiguous or untimely;

(iii) Fails to identify that a transaction has a profit-making motive where it is not already apparent from the context in which it is made.

From the above, it can be seen that it is no longer acceptable to rely upon a bold assertion that the relevant information was made available, though it was done late in the transactional process and effectively hidden in small print. There is a requirement to display information clearly and a commensurate recognition that obscure presentation of information is tantamount to an omission which is likely to be seen by the courts to be misleading in the context of CPUT.

SALES TACTICS

Sales is an increasingly complex and nuanced area of any business model whether the product is a tangible item or the provision of a service. It is a fact that the sales tactic deployed by the trader can greatly influence a consumer's decision and it would be naïve in the extreme to suggest that there is anything other than considerable reliance upon the material provided to a consumer in the sales process.

It is important to note that sales tactics which are designed to ensure that the real – or perhaps even arguably real – benefits of the product or service are sold as effectively as possible, are not the target of this area of the regulations. The intention is not to ensure that proactive selling, even that which might be annoying to some, become outlawed by the regulations. In fact, for the majority of 'hard sell' type traders, the CPUT regime should still not pose a problem because it is the occasion of excess in terms of behaviour which is envisaged as appropriately targeted by the regulations.

So for example, those traders that refuse to take no for an answer or refuse to leave a consumer's premises until a contract is signed and of course those who use threatening behaviour are likely to be committing an offence under the regulations. A commercial practice is outlawed if it is deemed to be aggressive and that should be determined by it using harassment, coercion or any degree of undue influence over the consumer. Further, if that sales tactic significantly impairs, or indeed if it is likely to significantly impair, the freedom of choice or conduct of the average consumer, then there is potentially a case to answer.

The follow-on point of course is if this action by the trader has then lead the consumer to take a transactional decision that they would not otherwise have made, and this point must always be carefully borne in mind by the practitioner constructing a case for prosecution or one establishing a defence case in these situations. There must have been a net effect in terms of the freedom of manoeuver of the consumer to make a transactional decision. To assist in assessing this, the legislation contains a list of criteria designed to help determine whether a given commercial practice uses harassment, coercion or undue influence. It is likely to be issues at the margins that cause the greatest difficulty because where, for example, the use of force can be evidence, then there is little difficulty in identifying coercion but where there is nothing apparently overt, greater care needs to be devoted to assessing what is the issue at hand.

Almost inevitably, the practitioner in this field will need to consider a multiplicity of factors in relation to the consumer, but their general disposition and certainly their age or any vulnerability will be important. It is a hackneyed but true characterization of many cases in this field that elderly consumers stand are far greater chance of falling victim to scams aimed at forcing them into a position where they do not feel able to say no to a sales pitch but it is vital that the general context is properly considered and assessed by the prosecuting or defending practitioner.

Undue influence is itself defined as "exploiting position of power to apply pressure even without using or threatening to use physical force, in a way which significantly limits the consumers ability to make an informed decision." Again we see this key factor at play; was the consumer's ability to make a free and fair decision in some way fettered by the manner in which the trader acted? If the answer to that question is yes, then there is likely to be case to answer in regards to the influence which has been exacted by the trader upon the consumer and, prima facie, there is a case to answer under CPUT.

It is crucial to recognise that in cases where a trader stands accused of having mislead consumers or of having acted in a way deemed to be aggressive, it is not enough for the prosecution to simply demonstrate that activity. In very many cases brought before the court, there can be a temptation to over emphasise the evidence on this point to the detriment of the overall case. A mainly criminal practitioner faced with needing to demonstrate for the prosecution of such a case, the exertion of undue influence on the consumer by the manner of visits, calls or contacts by the trader, may very well need to call witness evidence to establish this fact. The key point to recall is that once that act, or omission, is evidenced, it is crucial to then move on to what this has done to influence the consumer.

THE BLACKLIST OF BANNED PRACTICES

It is fair to say that up to this point in our analysis of the CPUT regime, a degree of analysis and assessment has been required and it is most likely that this will be the reality in very many cases. However, the potential practitioner in this field may be relieved to know that not all is a matter of nuance and interpretation because the regulations do list 31 specific practices which are banned and if there is evidence that one or more of these practices has been deployed by a trader, there is straightaway a case to answer. Of course it may very well be the case that there are a number of issues arising from one set of transactions both by means of misleading omissions and perhaps sales tactics or omissions but the welcome clarity of the black list provides something of a go-to benchmark for an analysis of a case at an early stage.

It is important to understand these blacklisted practices and how they can be evidenced and so it is worth looking in a little detail at the generality of the banned practices which make up the list.

BAIT ADVERTISING

This is where a practice is employed which lures consumers to a trader or to a potential transaction with the use of advertising around special, or limited time, price offers when it can be evidenced that the trader is aware they cannot offer that product or service or only has a few in stock at that price.

There are potentially very many possibly permutations of this but the key issues are often most likely to rotate around the knowledge of the trader; their must be knowledge on their part that the offer cannot be serviced in the overwhelming majority of cases. This may be harder to evidence than may at first blush appear to be the case as inefficiencies or poor stock monitoring can mean that a trader is in genuine ignorance of a capability which they are advertising but it is important that either circumstantially or directly, this knowledge is evidenced if there is to be a clear case to answer that the trader has indulged in bait advertising.

BAIT AND SWITCH

This second banned practice is closely tied to the first in terms of definition but might also be revealed by the evidence of bait advertising simpliciter so to speak. Bait and switch is the promotion of one product or service with the intention of selling you something else. Care must be taken here because it is not unusual, nor is it a blacklisted practice, to seek to sell a primary product but at the same time harbour the desire to sell an allied or linked product or service. So for example, when a car salesman advertises a car for sale whilst hoping that the consumer will enter into a lucrative finance deal with the trader as opposed to transacting a straightforward cash purchase, as long as the fundamental intention behind the advert for the car is to sell a car, no issue arises. Where the car serves purely as bait for a switch to a completely different product, then there may be an argument that this is a bait and switch occurrence.

Again, intention is crucial; it may be that during the course of discussions between the trader and consumer following the response to an advert for item or service A, it becomes clear that actually item or service B is a better prospect for the consumer. Equally, it might be that the terms of the deal on offer for product or service A are not as attractive to the consumer as the terms for product or service B. In that situation, it may be argued that what is at hand is a change of mind or a better deal.

The regulations are aimed clearly at situations in which the trader intends to switch the consumer to an alternative to that which is being advertised so that the product or service advertised is mere bait for the switch to the alternative, almost certainly more commercially propitious product.

LIMITED OFFERS

It is commonplace in all commercial marketplaces that some offers genuinely are limited either in terms of scope or temporally. There is nothing wrong with that and in real terms, it is highly unlikely that such offers can be seen as anything other than a staple of the marketplace. Where the banned practice comes into play is in the scenario where the trader has falsely stated that a product will only be available for a very limited period of time, or that it will only be available on particular items or services for a very limited time, in order to elicit an immediate decision and therefore to deprive consumers of a sufficient opportunity or time to make an informed choice.

There is a causative argument here; has the representation of the time limited nature of the offer had the effect of eliciting an immediate decision where there perhaps would not have been one? Crucially, has this acted so as to confine, unduly the room for thought and consideration which the consumer could have been expected to be afforded in the circumstances?

The limitation itself must of course be false and evidence should be adduced as to the knowledge of the trader at the time of the representation as well perhaps as of the reality of stock levels or the pertinent facts surrounding the item or service being offered for sale. In what is now becoming a well-trodden path of reasoning and logic, it is of course necessary to then also evidence the effect that this false representation had upon the consumer in terms of their decision making and the transaction that they have entered into.

FALSE FREE OFFERS

The essence of this particular area of banned practices is that if something is said to be free by the trader then it really must be free. That perhaps appears simplistic, but the reality must be that the item or service has no cost whatsoever attached to it. So if a product or service is described as free or as being without charge to the consumer but in order to obtain it, the consumer has to pay anything other than the unavoidable cost of responding to the offer and collecting or paying for the delivery of the item, then the practice is a banned one.

The key issue here is often clarity. If there are ensuing costs, they should be made clear and it is vital that the consumer is aware that what they are contracting for is not free; it may very well be cheaper than usual but it is not without cost. If the truth is that the consumer is going to find that they must outlay a cost when something is advertised as being a free offer, then the fact is that this is likely to be seen as a false free offer.

PRESSURE SELLING

Pressure in this context should not be seen as the sort of pressure that many consumers often impose upon themselves or those with them to transact a purchase but rather the creation by the trader of the impression that the consumer is obliged to form a contract. For example, at the extreme, creating the impression – whether implied or express – that the consumer may not leave until a contract is entered into, is quite clearly pressure selling.

It will not be at all unusual for a consumer to state that they felt pressured when hindsight means that a deal entered into has gone wrong or they are dissatisfied with the product but what we are concerned with here is something of a far greater order of magnitude. There needs to be quantifiable evidence that the trader has placed pressure upon the consumer to transact, albeit this pressure may vary from the extreme end of, for example, preventing them leaving the premises until the deal is done, through to the less acute of undue emphasis of the detriment of not carrying out the transaction. As ever, this will be a question of varying evidence in different cases, but it is important to be aware that pressure can come in a very wide range of forms.

AGGRESSIVE DOORSTEP SELLING

The practice of doorstep selling is perhaps far less frequent than it once was and there is a specific trade association which is in place for many practitioners of this form of sales, the Direct Selling Association (DSA). Membership is not mandatory but if a supplier is a member of the DSA and is found to be in breach of their code, there are sanctions which mean that a trader can be forced to repay any money received fro the consumers, repair or replace a faulty item which they have provided for no cost or, in the ultimate sanction, pay compensation of up to £5,000.

The essence of the prohibitions here relate to doorstep selling which, as the category refers to, is aggressive. Often this might take the form of the trader, or their representatives, making personal visits to the consumers home and ignoring requests to leave or not to return. The degree of persistence here and perhaps the tone and manner of the visits will be important because the yardstick of note will vary from one consumer to another. It is not difficult to see how some consumers would find visits from traders to be intimidating whereas a neighbour receiving the same visit from the same trader, may be undaunted by it.

Again, there are certain practices within this which are clearly infringements; if there is evidence of direct requests to the trader from the consumer that they do not visit in person, or that they cease to do so having already called, but the trader persists in the conduct which they have been asked to refrain from, it becomes easier to argue that their behaviour is aggressive. It is important to note that this area is aimed at aggressive doorstep *selling* and should not be confused with practices employed by debt collectors when a consumer has refused to pay a trader and lawful enforcement has been commenced. It is not uncommon in this scenario for an aggrieved consumer who, for whatever reason has refused to pay some or all of the sums outstanding, to then make a complaint because they have received visits to seek to recover monies.

This may well still amount to a practice which requires investigation and perhaps even sanction, but the reality of this area of the CPUT blacklist is it is aimed at the beginning rather than the end of the transactional process; it is focused on the manner and the efforts made by the trader to bring about the contract or agreement in the first place, not the measures and steps taken to seek satisfaction of their demands for payment later on.

TRADING WITHIN THE EU

As we have already seen, the CPUT regulations implemented the European Unfair Commercial Practices Directive[32] which was aimed at providing clarity to consumers of what their rights were whilst simultaneously simplifying the process of trading within the EU as part of the single market. That directive provides to consumers in England and Wales the same protection from unfair practices and rogue traders whether the transaction is with a physical shop a mile away from the home of the consumer or through a website based in Spain or Greece.

Anyone looking at a product or service widely available for purchase online in the modern world will almost certainly find that they are actually trading with an entity which in some way has part of its operation outside the UK and when that is within the EU, it means that there is potential protection for the consumer to be derived from the Directive. This is not a one-way process though and whilst it is fair to say that the framing of much of the wording of the directive and the CPUT regulations which derive from it are couched very much in a way which imposes duties on the trader and rights on the consumer, there are reciprocal benefits to the trader.

A business is now able to advertise and market to consumers in the EU in the same way that they do to domestic customers and that opens up the ability of a company or trader based in England and Wales to trade with consumers across the EU just as the reverse is true. At the time of writing, the UK is undergoing the process of departure from the EU but it is hard to see how any putative trade deal between the EU and the UK will not in some way passport the requirements of the directive and current regulations so that trading can continue post Brexit.

The regulations continue to apply during the transition period and it is worth simply noting that the principle aim of both the directive and

---

[32] Ibid, (2005/29/EC)

then its domestic interpretation, CPUT, is the boosting of consumer confidence and the giving to businesses of all sizes, a uniform and transparent EU wide set of rules for their transactions.

RIGHT TO REDRESS

CPUT provides several general rights to redress for the consumer and it is important that the practitioner is aware of these at the point of conducting litigation. In and of themselves, the way in which the trader and consumer have operated may very well provide ground for issues which form litigation, but they are aimed at providing a series of mechanisms for unwinding a problem and diffusing what could otherwise be a costly outstanding dispute.

The rights which CPUT provides fall into three key areas;

A right to undo the contract.

CPUT provides effectively for a cooling off period of 90 days in which the contract can be brought to an end and a refund obtained. The time scales are crucial here and it must be borne in mind that this 90-day limit will start on the latest of four points.

Firstly, the date at which the contract was entered into, secondly, from when the goods, digital content or services were received, thirdly from when the lease began (if the contract amounts to a lease) and, finally; from the point at which the consumers right of cancellation is first exercisable.

In many cases, it should be relatively easy to ascertain the relevant dates and timeframes and perhaps if there is a dispute or uncertainty about this, as well as potentially being a matter of evidence, it may be said that any uncertainty as a result of opaque contractual terms can itself give rise to a suggestion that there has been a CPUT breach.

Importantly, a refund can only be received by the consumer in the event that they have not fully consumed the goods, digital products or they have not received the contracted for service in full. It is no good having completely concluded the use or consumption of a product to then demand a refund for it; this is based on the premise that when there is a point reached at which the consumer can say there has been dissatisfaction in some shape or form, they should seek redress and may then expect a refund.

Closely allied to this, is the expectation that goods supplied to the consumer which now form part of a request for a refund are made available for collection by the trader. It is not unusual that a potentially aggrieved consumer may feel the need to retain possession of an arguably faulty product as some form of insurance against a lack of refund from the trader. It is crucial that the trader have made available to them those goods for collection by the trader.

In the event that the contract has been paid for through a finance agreement and that contract was made as a result of either aggressive selling or misleading selling, then the contract can be exited by the consumer and anything paid by them can be recouped, effectively resetting the clock to zero and putting the consumer – and the trader – back to the position in which they were in prior to the arrangements having been made.

A right to a discount on the price paid

The consumer will be able to seek a discount in respect of past or future payments which fall due under the contract. It was often commonplace before the imposition of the CPUT regime for there to be disputes as to quantum when it came to discounts even when the fact of a proposed discount may not have been in dispute. This was for obvious commercial reasons with the consumer wanting as close to 100% of the price refunded and the trader wanting as close to 0% refunded, leading to an inexorable tension between the two positions.

CPUT stipulates the regime to be employed in these situations. Where the value of the contract is £5,000 or less, there is an entitlement of the consumer to 25%, 50%, 75% or 100%. Those percentages are anchored to the nature of the breach by the trader, so the percentage attaches to whether the breach is minor, significant or very serious.

Where the contractual value is more than £5,000 there is an entitlement of the consumer to a figure which represents the extent to which the price of the contract exceeded the market price. In other words, the overcharge on the contract when set against the market price for the same product, service or digital contract.

The determinant of the level of seriousness will be dependent upon the behaviour of the trader, the impact it has on the consumer and the length of time which has passed since the contract was signed by the consumer. Again, these points are likely to be matters of evidence in each individual case and there will be a different position in relation to each case for a wide-ranging number of reasons.

An entitlement to seek damages

In the event that the consumer has incurred a financial loss which they would not have had to bear but for the actions of the trader, then prima facie there will be a possibility that the consumer can make a claim for damages. This is not an exclusive proposition because CPUT provides for the aggrieved consumer in this position to make a claim for damages which sits alongside choosing to receive a discount or cancelling the contract.

A claim can be made not simply in the case that there has been a financial loss. Where it can be demonstrated that the consumer has suffered alarm, distress or either physical inconvenience or discomfort and this was a result of the trader's actions, then there will potentially be an entitlement on the part of the consumer to damages from the trader.

Whether prosecuting or defending a matter in this area, it is important to note that a trader would have a defence to many of the offences set out in the CPUT regulations if they are able to demonstrate that their actions – or omissions –were a result of an accident, a mistake, the act or default of someone else, information which was supplied by another person or a general catchall of factors which were outside of their control.

Given the often complex nature of many contemporary transactions, it is not difficult to see how these defences can be very real prospects in many cases and the practitioner will need to thoroughly understand the complexion of the representations and decisions which form the transactional process for the trader. No matter how professional a trader may seek to be or how sophisticated their operation may actually be, it is not difficult to see how accidents and mistakes can happen and it is vital to understand the processes involved whether one is appearing for the trader or the consumer.

However, traders can only rely on such defences if they can evidence that they took reasonable precautions to prevent accidents or mistakes from occurring and that they exercised all due diligence to avoid committing an offence. As ever, ignorance may be an explanation but it most certainly is not a defence and the trader who finds themselves being prosecuted must be prepared to provide information that they did exercise all due diligence and had steps in place to prevent accidents or errors taking place wherever possible.

OTHER IMPORTANT FACTORS WITH RIGHT TO REDRESS

This set of rights is a qualified one and they are completely predicated on there being a contract which has been entered into by the consumer. There is a key difference here with the rest of the regulations because under the wider CPUT regime, it is enough simply for the consumer to show that they have taken some kind of transactional decision, like entering a retailed because of a misleading advertisement. The right to redress is founded on the transaction having more substance to it than that and a contact must have been formed.

The misleading action of the trader must have been a significant factor in the entry into the contract. If the consumer has entered the contract as a direct result of the misleading action of the trader or as a result of aggressive selling, it will be necessary for this to be demonstrated as at leas a significant factor in the consumer's decision to enter into that contract. The significance of this as a factor will be a key determinant of a right to redress.

Finally, the right to redress pertains to positive acts by the trader, so a misleading action is covered by the right to redress, as is a case of aggressive selling of course, but an omission which is misleading is not covered. Again, the distinction can be a fine one but it is important to see the right of the consumer as being linked to a positive act by the trader which can be highlighted rather than simply an omission. However, that does not of course preclude the bringing of charges under other areas of CPUT; it is simply a qualification of the general right of redress under the regulations.

THE TRADE DESCRIPTIONS ACT 1968

The protection of consumers is something which today is very much framed by legislation which has arisen over the last decade or so, but it would be wrong to attribute consumer protection legislation simply to the legislation which has come about since the globalized economy became a reality. The problem of rogue traders and disputes between traders and consumers is as old as commerce itself and it is possible to delve very deep into history and still unearth varied rules and regulations put in place with an eye to trying to regulate commerce in some way. The harsh reality of commerce, old and new, is that there will always be individuals and organisations who are seeking to take advantage of others for profit and to that end the problem at which all legislation is addressed, can be seen as an extension of the human condition and not just a product of the modern world and modern trade.

The Trade Descriptions Act 1968 came into effect on 30th November 1968 and replaced the Merchandise Marks Act by providing a general expansion of coverage from the MMA. It was the Trade Descriptions Act which made it an offence for a trader to sell a product based on misinformation and the aim of the Act was to compel traders to act more truthfully and transparently about the product or service they were supplying. It sought to prevent a trader from deliberately misleading a consumer and from bringing about a situation in which the consumer spend money on a false claim.

Importantly, the Act gave the courts the power to impose penalties on offending traders who were making false claims of their products and there was the ancillary power to confiscate from the trader, goods and products related to the product or service. For the first time, fines could be imposed upon traders who had acted in a way that brought them into breach of the Act.

Largely, the Trade Descriptions Act 1968 has been superseded by the CPUT regulations but it can be seen that in the evolution of the current framework, the Act laid much of the foundation for what was to come. In many respects therefore the CPUT regime, though directly deriving from a European Directive, built upon the Trade Descriptions Act by including wording about false endorsements and other pressure or aggressive sales tactics.

The Act is still valid but is likely that actions brought against traders and by consumers will be founded in the CPUT regime rather than the Act of 1968. That said, for those wishing to understand the purpose of the CPUT regulations and the issues of false representations and certain tactics by traders, no understanding of the contemporary picture is complete without some recognition of the role that the Trade Descriptions Act 1968 played in the regulatory landscape which today applies.

PART TWO

COMPLIANCE AND ENFORCEMENT

CHAPTER SIX

GENERAL ENFORCEMENT

There is a general duty upon Trading Standards (and in Northern Irelands, the Department of Enterprise, Trade and Investment) to enforce the terms of the CPUT regime. Of course, the decision as to whether there should be action and what guise that action should take, whether criminal or civil, is a matter for decisions in each specific case and the legislation does not dictate the avenue which those pursuing these matters should go down. There is of course no reason why enforcement action, whether civil or criminal, must be taken in respect of each individual infringement of the rules and the key emphasis should always be on achieving compliance with the legislation.

It is right at this point that the practitioner involved in such a case should pause for thought. If prosecuting such a case, there should be real consideration given to this as if it were an overriding objective; is it the case that the trader has been encouraged to comply with their obligations and can it be seen that Trading Standards are acting as a 'fair minded minister of justice"? That test, familiar to all who prosecute criminal matters in the Magistrates' and Crown Court is one that those tasked with prosecuting a CPUT matter would do well to observe, simply because of the panoply of tools at the disposal of the putative prosecutor. To put the matter simply, it may be that the breach of CPUT which is at hand is one that need not automatically result in enforcement action; all of the options should be weighed and balanced.

Similarly, on the other side of the coin, the defendant in such a case should not presume that enforcement will not flow from a breach simply because it may be the first or relatively minor in their eyes. These are judgments which require the evidence and surrounding circumstances to be carefully balanced. What is key is that those tasked with enforcement should promote compliance by the most appropriate means and should do so in line with their own enforcement policies.

Broadly speaking, those tasked with enforcement have a range of tools at their disposal to ensure traders are complying with the CPUT regime. These fall into five main categories;

1) Education, advice or guidance
2) Established means;
3) Codes of Conduct (where applicable)
4) Civil enforcement action
5) Criminal enforcement – prosecution.

It has already been noted that the decisions as to which approach to take will vary from one case to another and the decision-making process may not be straightforward. The variable nature of the issues at hand will call for an equally variable set of approaches and it would be both wrong and implausible to try and set out the ideal, or even a recommended methodology.

However what must always be the case is that those assessing such matters must have clear regard to principles of proportionality, accountability and consistence. They should also be transparent in their targeting and where formal enforcement action is deemed necessary, this should have clear aims in mind.

Firstly, the behaviour of the offender is the clear target; those tasked with enforcement of CPUT matters should be seeking to change the behaviour of the offender. That may be more or less straight forward depending on the case, but it will always need to be clear in the enforcers mind. Allied to this, a principal objective will be to remove any financial benefit or gain which appears to exist through non-compliance. Put simply, it will need to be made clear that compliance is a wiser option that the financial gains of not complying with CPUT.

The enforcer will need to be pragmatic and should consider what is appropriate for the specific case. Not all offenders warrant the same approach and again, it is wise to be mindful of the need to tailor the response to the case.

There should be a proportionate enforcement response. That proportionality should be achieved by measuring the response against the nature of the offence and the harm which has been caused. Fourthly, where harm has been caused by the regulatory non-compliance, this should be rectified if both possible and appropriate. Finally, there need to be a deterrence aimed at further non-compliance; there is little point in enforcement action of any type which does not act so as to deter that offender – or others – from similar activity.

Those enforcing CPUT matters much ensure that they are acting in accordance with the Regulators' Compliance Code and should measure their actions and decisions against this.[33] What will be apparent, not just from the Code but also from an assessment of the situation in general is that enforcers should seek to try and obtain compliance in the first instance by the giving of education and advice in the initial instance of a breach. It may very well be that this resolves the matter but there is no requirement that things cannot progress more quickly; if the situation and circumstances require it, then immediate enforcement action maybe required and that can include criminal investigation and prosecution.

---

[33] The Regulators' Compliance Code applies to the enforcement of CPUT in England, Scotland and Wales but not in Northern Ireland where the protection of consumers is a devolved matter. Section 24(3) Legislative and Regulatory Reform Act 2006 and Article 4 of The Legislative and Regulatory Reform (Regulatory Functions) Order 2007, SI 2007/3544.

CHAPTER SEVEN

CODES OF CONDUCT AND CIVIL ENFORCEMENT

There are various occasions in which it may be deemed unnecessary for intervention by Trading Standards to take place at all, if for example the trader is having the complaint investigated by other means of regulatory overview or regulator. If Trading Standards enforcers are happy that the issues are being dealt with by other systems and the complaints fall within the scope of other mechanisms, they may take a decision that there is no requirement for them to step in and carry out enforcement action. That is not to say that they are barred from doing so nor that enforcement cannot be a multi handed event, but if the matter is being dealt with under an established code type regulatory, it may be that further enforcement becomes either otiose or disproportionate.

The relationship between enforcers can be either exclusive or symbiotic. In appropriate cases, enforcers are entitled to seek to enlist the help of those with responsibility for self regulatory codes of conduct and it is not difficult to see how a two-way movement of information and investigation can lead to a more holistic solution for all concerned. Equally, it may mean that the proportionality of a trading standards type investigation stays in clearer relief.

Equally, a trader who has agreed to be bound by the terms of a self regulatory code of conduct may find that they have breached CPUT by failing in their commitments in the code. This is especially so if the trader has indicated in a commercial practice that they are bound by the code and importantly, if the transactional decisions of the consumer are likely to be impacted by this.

With regard to this, is should be noted that in such a case, enforcement will be by way of injunctive civil actions and not criminal proceedings. Enforcers can take civil action when there are CPUT breaches and a number of bodies are empowered to take such enforcement actions. The upshot of that process is that enforcers apply to the courts for an enforcement order preventing infringements. Breaching of such an order could be seen as a contempt of court and if that is so, can lead to imprisonment of up to two years and/or an unlimited fine.

As in all areas however, the enforcers should seek to stop an infringement by embarking upon consultation with the trader before applying to the court for an enforcement order. It may very well be that through this process, it becomes unnecessary for an order to be sought or instead of an order being obtained an acceptable undertaking might be obtainable which would see the trader commit not to engage in or repeat the previous conduct which constituted a breach of infringement. The graduated approach can be seen again but this shouldn't be thought of simply as a matter of policy or process. A trader who continues in breach behaviour having given an undertaking will find defending such proceedings in the future more difficult and the likelihood of Trading Standards succeeding in their action is increased commensurately.

There are other advantages here for enforcers as a court has the ability to order a trader to produce evidence to substantiate a factual claim which they may make in a commercial practice. This may very well serve to truncate matters if the trader either cannot produce such evidence or if, on production, it does not evidence what it was thought to.

CHAPTER EIGHT

CRIMINAL OFFENCES AND INVESTIGATIVE POWERS

Criminal prosecutions under the CPUT regime are primarily brought by trading standards on behalf of aggrieved complainants and so the cases are effectively prosecuted by local authorities before the Magistrates and Crown Court. By their very nature, many of these prosecutions will have been bought because all earlier efforts to dissuade the trader from such breaches have failed or simply because the nature of the breach is so serious or egregious, that criminal prosecution has had to be resorted to.

There are a number of specific offences;

(i) contravention of the requirements of the general prohibition

(ii) misleading actions (except 5(3)(b) code commitments)

(iii) misleading omissions (including the omission of specified information in invitations to purchase)

(iv) aggressive practices

(v) specific unfair commercial practices.

All of these offences are strict liability though the contravention of the general prohibition requires proof of mens rea. Often, a charge sheet or indictment will feature a range of matters and the practitioner taking hold of a case for the first time will need to be aware that the charges which can flow from essentially the same activity – or omission – can be numerous. If the conduct of the trader has been repeated with a number of consumers, as is typically the case, then the trader can expect to face individual charges or counts in relation to each one or each transaction.

Obviously, in terms of the strict liability offences, in these cases all that the prosecution need to is to prove that there has been a prohibited act or omission. In that sense, the issue is likely to be a narrow one though may require evidence in a limited form. The state of mind of the defendant trader is irrelevant to those breaches but it may very well be that alongside those charges appear allegations of breaches of the general prohibition and these do of course require a particular state of mind to be evidenced; whether it was clear knowledge of the issue or recklessness in engaging in a commercial practice which fails to comply with the requirement of professional diligence.

As mentioned earlier, it is equally possible that a comprehensive charge sheet or indictment will encapsulate these various CPUT offences, potentially in some numbers if there have been a number of complainants or a range of possible breaches but the charge sheet might also contain other offences, such as fraud. So at the point that the practitioner receives the brief to prosecute or defence a criminal prosecution under CPUT, they should expect to have to think in several directions simultaneously; the points to prove and the defence to advance will have to cover a number of issues which need to be borne in mind.

In terms of the general prohibition and prosecutions for contravening this, the mens rea need only be shown in relation to the contravention of the requirements of professional diligence and this is that the trader new this to be the case or was reckless as to whether it was the fact. There is no need at this point for the prosecutor to show this in relation to the effects on the average consumer when they are assessed against both the material distortion and transactional decision concepts.

BODIES CORPORATE

Increasingly, the courts are having to deal with cases in which a body corporate commits an offence with the consent perhaps of a guiding mind, or an officer of that body. In those cases, both the officer and the corporate body can be prosecuted and sentenced and it is increasingly rare that the prosecuting authorities will allow the pleas to be loaded onto the body corporate to facilitate the individual escaping sanction, or vice versa. The same considerations apply where the commission of the offence is due to neglect on the part of that officer.

ACTS OF OTHERS

If an individual commits an offence under the CPUT regime, and the commission of that offence is due to the act or even the default of another individual, then they too can face proceedings and that is irrelevant of whether action is brought against the original individual offender.

Prosecutions under CPUT are subject to time limits and those prosecuting these matters, or those who advise them, must ensure that the prosecution is brought either within three years of the offence taking place or within 12 months of the discovery of the alleged offence by the prosecutor; whichever is earlier. Again, this is a prescient consideration for those defending as there can be cases where because of the complexities which might be involved, proceedings are actually not initiated within the time frames stipulated. Those prosecuting – just as in a private prosecution – should be mindful of the time limits and because of the nature of these type of cases, should be prepared to assist the court in questions as to these matters. Even though there is a growing number of such cases, it is still right to say that the courts are not overly familiar with the requirements and it will be the case that input from those representing should be offered throughout.

DEFENCES

As has been discussed, the vast majority of CPUT offences are matters of strict liability and in those cases the only defences are due diligence and innocent publication. Those defending will need to make the usual judgment call in these scenarios as to whether an explanation advanced by a defendant trader amounts to due diligence or innocent publication or whether it is more properly mitigation.

Due diligence can be relied upon for offences of misleading actions or omissions, aggressive commercial practices and specific unfair commercial practices. In these cases if the defence of due diligence is to be successfully raised then the trader must prove that the commission of the offence was attributable to a mistake, reliance on information given by another person, the act or default of another, an accident or some other cause which was beyond their control. Not only that, but once such a category is identified, the defendant trader will need to evidence that they took all reasonable precautions and exercised all due diligence in order to avoid committing the offence, or to avoid someone under his control committing it.

These are tall evidential orders and whilst they may be the subject of witness testimony assertion, it is paramount that they are evidenced properly if the defence is to succeed. Of course, before the criminal courts, a defence point need be proven to the lower – civil – burden. Nonetheless, there is a considerable amount of work to do to set out and effectively evidence the defence if it is to be relied upon.

Procedurally, the enforcement body must be given written notice of a defence which is based upon the actions of a third party and this must be done seven days before any court hearing. It is not enough to show that due diligence procedures were in place; the application of those procedures in practice will be necessary. Proportionality plays a part here and whilst there is nothing specific to require it, in truth the courts are likely to place greater expectations here on a larger business or operation than upon a smaller trading entity.

Alternatively, innocent publication can be relied upon as a defence in cases which include advertisements. The trader who wishes to avail themselves of this defence in relation to offences of misleading actions or omissions, aggressive commercial practices and specific unfair commercial practices, will have to prove that they are a person whose business it is to either publish or arrange for the publications of adverts. Further, they will need to prove that they received the advertisement in the ordinary course of their business. Again the manner of approach to this may be different dependent on the size of the business and the sort of formalities which surround the operation of larger entities in contrast with smaller trading outfits.

Finally, they would need to prove that they neither knew nor had reason to know that the publication would amount to an offence.

INVESTIGATIVE POWERS

The originator of the powers currently enjoyed by Trading Standards in the investigation of CPUT offences is the Trade Descriptions Act 1968 as it was from this act that most of those powers originated, though they have been considerably modernized and updated to deal with a far more complex trading landscape than existed at the close of the 1960's.

The Trade Descriptions Act relied heavily upon test purchases of products and whilst the reliance placed on this technique by Trading Standards is not quite as it was previously, enforcement officers are empowered to check CPUT compliance by purchasing products to test, or to secure the provision of those products.

It should be emphasized that in large numbers of cases enforcement techniques insofar as the obtaining of evidence and information is concerned are relatively straightforward. This will often be because of consumers coming forward with their own complaints and information or other agencies notifying Trading Standards of potential breaches. However, where necessary, enforcement officers can enter premises and are able at all reasonable hours and without a warrant to;

1) inspect goods and to enter premises which are not only used as a dwelling, in order to ascertain whether a breach has been committed;

2) require traders to produce any documentation in relation to their business and this includes those held on computerized devices. Additionally, they can take copies and require that documents be produced to them in legible form, if they have reasonable cause to suspect that a breach has been committed in order to ascertain whether this is the cause;

3) seize and detain goods if they have reasonable cause to believe that a breach has been committed in order to ascertain, by testing for example, whether this is the case.

Additionally, enforcement officers have the power to seize goods or documentation without a warrant if they have reason to believe that they may in due course be required as evidence in proceedings against that person for a breach. In some cases, that power may include the power to break into items or containers so as to obtain the items.

With a warrant, enforcement officers can enter a dwelling. Such a warrant can only be granted by the Magistrates' Court when that court is satisfied that there are reasonable grounds for believing that certain conditions are met. Those conditions are that there are goods or documents in that dwelling which an enforcement body has the power to inspect. Further, it must also be the case that their inspection is likely to disclose evidence of a CPUT breach, whether that breach has occurred in the past, is currently being committed or may be about to be committed.

Secondly, with a warrant they can enter a dwelling if their admission has either already been refused or is likely to be refused and – probably in light of that – a notice of intention to apply for a warrant has been given. In the alternative, if applying for admission, or giving a notice of intention to apply for a warrant would serve to defeat the objective of the entry, then the reasonable grounds will likely have been met.

The enforcement officer who gains entry to a premises with a warrant, is required to produce this to the occupier of the premises when they have done so. In certain cases, especially if there is a fear of a breach of the peace, the police are likely to be in attendance but their role is limited to one of ensuring that no criminality occurs and is not part of the search process.

Once an enforcement officer has gained entry, whether or not this is under a warrant, they may take with them any persons or equipment that they believe is necessary for that purpose. So it will not be unusual for a relatively large number of individuals to turn up at a premises to carry out a search. These powers are available whether civil or criminal proceedings are in mind or take place but if these powers are used by Trading Standards for criminal proceedings, they must comply with the Police and Criminal Evidence Act 1984

The obligations of the enforcement agent do not end with the commission of the search. In specific circumstances, they are under an obligation to notify a trader of the results of any tests which are subsequently conducted on goods which have either been seized or purchased pursuant to their powers of investigation. If those goods are lost, damaged or in some other way made to deteriorate, the owners of those goods may be compensated. That requirement extends only so far as there has been no breach of the CPUT and the seizure is not due to the negligence or default by the person concerned.

PENALTIES

As at the time of writing, there are no Sentencing Guidelines in place for the sentencing of CPUT matters but in general terms, summary convictions for such matters will result in a fine that does not exceed the statutory maximum. However conviction on indictment will lead to a fine or imprisonment not exceeding two years, or both.

CHAPTER NINE

CONCLUSION

As can be seen from Part 1 of this book, the law developed in this area from a number of sources and over a period of time. It would be fair to say that for the most part, it was the case that this area was one which was largely civil in its nature and conception but that over time, in large part due to the influence of policy considerations which sought to enshrine wider public policy doctrines, this area of law became one that can be as litigated before the criminal courts as the civil courts.

Whatever the history here, the contemporary reality is that traders are now bound by a panoply of legislative measures which are as likely to be enforced through the criminal courts as the civil and that brings with it very different considerations to those that would perhaps have been deployed in this field some years ago. Regulatory work is becoming an increasingly important part of many practitioner's diaries. For the reasons that were set out in the introduction, it is important to recognise that the historically clear categories of legal practice are not as clear as they once were. Hopefully, the proceeding pages have shown that taking a practical approach to the regulatory and criminal side of consumer protection legislation and the CPUT regime, requires an understanding of the civil methodology surround enforcement as well.

The landscape of this legislation is a complex one and the texture of the approach taken to enforcement is commensurately complicated. We can see that the direction of travel for policy makers has been toward greater rights for consumers and correspondingly greater obligations for traders. That is something that began at a pan-European level but was embraced and enshrined with alacrity by English policy makers and legislators. At the time of writing, the UK is days away from leaving the European Union, with or without a deal, but there is nothing to suggest that once that departure is concluded, the reach of these policy issues will in any way be lessened. It is quire clear that the cause of consumer rights and protection and of obligations upon traders has become very much a domestic cause, notwithstanding its continental antecedents.

Whatever may be thought about the regulatory burden upon traders or about the mechanisms of enforcement of regulations, the genie is out of the bottle and in the opinion of the author, the reality is that the scope of the current regulations will not diminish. If anything, we can see that the desire of consumers to know that the force of the law is with them, has grown rather than diminished. The nature of the trading relationships which consumers enter into has become more complex over time and if anything, the pace of change means that is likely to continue to be the case. As that happens, consumers will want and need to be able to enforce their rights through civil actions but they are also likely to find that Trading Standards and others seek to enforce matters through the criminal courts so as to maximise the likelihood of preventing such future breaches.

At the time of writing the UK, and much of the world, is gripped by the Covid-19 pandemic. It is already becoming clear that this has altered peoples trading behaviour and has undoubtedly impacted the way in which consumers interact with those from whom they purchase goods, services and digital content. Perhaps it is actually more accurate to say that the pandemic has increased the speed at which their behaviour was already changing. In its turn, that will have given rise to errors and breaches, some more innocent than others, and that in its turn will certainly see an increase in these matters coming before various courts.

The nature of legal practice has also been impacted by Covid but again, perhaps the changes which are beginning to be seen were ones which were always going to come about but the pace of their implementation has quickened. The profession is undergoing various changes but key to all of that is likely to be a need not just for specialization but for a blurring of the lines between categories. Traders faced with smaller profits because of less footfall are likely to want to go to a legal representative who can at the very least provide them with clear guidance on both the civil and the criminal implications of the issues they are grappling with.

With local authority budgets likely to come under strain, Trading Standards may wish to be advised and represented not by a raft of lawyers each bringing their own expertise, albeit in a silo, to the case but rather by someone who appears to be an expert generalist. That phrase might sound contradictory, but on reflection in terms of the legislation in this area and looking at the realities we all now face in a very changed and fast changing world, it become a clear and present reality.

Given all of that, practitioners who come from one side or the other of the civil- criminal divide, are likely to find themselves contesting cases on very similar ground to one another. It is possible that the category 'regulatory' will gain a greater traction and become its one defined group in a far more established way, but whatever the changes that are to come, it seems inescapable that in this area, we will all need to develop a practical understanding of the realities of practice across the range of civil and criminal law. Hard cases may make bad law as the saying goes, but cases with blurred lines may make future law.

What can be said with certainty is that traders and consumers will continue to interact and to do so in an ever more complex manner. That will inevitably give rise to disputes and for several decades now, it can be seen that policy makers have chosen to respond to the call for greater communication with greater enforceable regulation for traders. In the context of the law of England and Wales, that has left a situation where cases can, and are, determined in both the criminal and civil jurisdiction.

It is inconceivable that one or other of those jurisdictions will cease to address these problems because they truly sit astride the two areas of practice. The obvious corollary of that is that whilst categorization has been something we have hung onto in the legal profession in a self defining way for decades, in the fields of consumer legislation generally and its enforcement specifically, we need to be prepared to recognise that whichever side we represent, we will need to take a practical as well as a holisitic approach. For the erstwhile criminal practitioner that will mean a growing need to understand the civil implications attached to a case and vice versa. It is fair to go as far as to say that any approach which seeks to look solely at one area or the other is at best, half the picture.

This is an area of law which has evolved steadily over the years, deriving from EU directives transplanted into English law. The departure of the UK from the EU is unlikely to see a change in the growth of the general consumer rights movement and that in turn means that we can expect litigation to be an inevitable side effect of that policy development.

If this practical guide assists in widening the approach taken by those involved in these cases, it will have done its job.

MORE BOOKS BY LAW BRIEF PUBLISHING

A selection of our other titles available now:-

'A Practical Guide to Solicitor and Client Costs – 2nd Edition' by Robin Dunne
'Constructive Dismissal – Practice Pointers and Principles' by Benjimin Burgher
'A Practical Guide to Religion and Belief Discrimination Claims in the Workplace' by Kashif Ali
'A Practical Guide to the Law of Medical Treatment Decisions' by Ben Troke
'Fundamental Dishonesty and QOCS in Personal Injury Proceedings: Law and Practice' by Jake Rowley
'A Practical Guide to the Law in Relation to School Exclusions' by Charlotte Hadfield & Alice de Coverley
'A Practical Guide to Divorce for the Silver Separators' by Karin Walker
'The Right to be Forgotten – The Law and Practical Issues' by Melissa Stock
'A Practical Guide to Planning Law and Rights of Way in National Parks, the Broads and AONBs' by James Maurici QC, James Neill et al
'A Practical Guide to Election Law' by Tom Tabori
'A Practical Guide to the Law in Relation to Surrogacy' by Andrew Powell
'A Practical Guide to Claims Arising from Fatal Accidents – 2nd Edition' by James Patience
'A Practical Guide to the Ownership of Employee Inventions – From Entitlement to Compensation' by James Tumbridge & Ashley Roughton
'A Practical Guide to Asbestos Claims' by Jonathan Owen & Gareth McAloon
'A Practical Guide to Stamp Duty Land Tax in England and Northern Ireland' by Suzanne O'Hara
'A Practical Guide to the Law of Farming Partnerships' by Philip Whitcomb

'Covid-19, Homeworking and the Law – The Essential Guide to Employment and GDPR Issues' by Forbes Solicitors
'Covid-19, Force Majeure and Frustration of Contracts – The Essential Guide' by Keith Markham
'Covid-19 and Criminal Law – The Essential Guide' by Ramya Nagesh
'Covid-19 and Family Law in England and Wales – The Essential Guide' by Safda Mahmood
'A Practical Guide to the Law of Unlawful Eviction and Harassment – 2nd Edition' by Stephanie Lovegrove
'Covid-19, Residential Property, Equity Release and Enfranchisement – The Essential Guide' by Paul Sams and Louise Uphill
'Covid-19, Brexit and the Law of Commercial Leases – The Essential Guide' by Mark Shelton
'A Practical Guide to Costs in Personal Injury Claims – 2nd Edition' by Matthew Hoe
'A Practical Guide to the General Data Protection Regulation (GDPR) – 2nd Edition' by Keith Markham
'Ellis on Credit Hire – Sixth Edition' by Aidan Ellis & Tim Kevan
'A Practical Guide to Working with Litigants in Person and McKenzie Friends in Family Cases' by Stuart Barlow
'Protecting Unregistered Brands: A Practical Guide to the Law of Passing Off' by Lorna Brazell
'A Practical Guide to Secondary Liability and Joint Enterprise Post-Jogee' by Joanne Cecil & James Mehigan
'A Practical Guide to the Pre-Action RTA Claims Protocol for Personal Injury Lawyers' by Antonia Ford
'A Practical Guide to Neighbour Disputes and the Law' by Alexander Walsh
'A Practical Guide to Forfeiture of Leases' by Mark Shelton
'A Practical Guide to Coercive Control for Legal Practitioners and Victims' by Rachel Horman

'A Practical Guide to Rights Over Airspace and Subsoil' by Daniel Gatty
'Tackling Disclosure in the Criminal Courts – A Practitioner's Guide' by Narita Bahra QC & Don Ramble
'A Practical Guide to the Law of Driverless Cars – Second Edition' by Alex Glassbrook, Emma Northey & Scarlett Milligan
'A Practical Guide to TOLATA Claims' by Greg Williams
'Artificial Intelligence – The Practical Legal Issues' by John Buyers
'A Practical Guide to the Law of Prescription in Scotland' by Andrew Foyle
'A Practical Guide to the Construction and Rectification of Wills and Trust Instruments' by Edward Hewitt
'A Practical Guide to the Law of Bullying and Harassment in the Workplace' by Philip Hyland
'How to Be a Freelance Solicitor: A Practical Guide to the SRA-Regulated Freelance Solicitor Model' by Paul Bennett
'A Practical Guide to Prison Injury Claims' by Malcolm Johnson
'A Practical Guide to the Small Claims Track' by Dominic Bright
'A Practical Guide to Advising Clients at the Police Station' by Colin Stephen McKeown-Beaumont
'A Practical Guide to Antisocial Behaviour Injunctions' by Iain Wightwick
'Practical Mediation: A Guide for Mediators, Advocates, Advisers, Lawyers, and Students in Civil, Commercial, Business, Property, Workplace, and Employment Cases' by Jonathan Dingle with John Sephton
'The Mini-Pupillage Workbook' by David Boyle
'A Practical Guide to Crofting Law' by Brian Inkster
'A Practical Guide to Spousal Maintenance' by Liz Cowell
'A Practical Guide to the Law of Domain Names and Cybersquatting' by Andrew Clemson
'A Practical Guide to the Law of Gender Pay Gap Reporting' by Harini Iyengar

'A Practical Guide to the Rights of Grandparents in Children Proceedings' by Stuart Barlow
'NHS Whistleblowing and the Law' by Joseph England
'Employment Law and the Gig Economy' by Nigel Mackay & Annie Powell
'A Practical Guide to Noise Induced Hearing Loss (NIHL) Claims' by Andrew Mckie, Ian Skeate, Gareth McAloon
'An Introduction to Beauty Negligence Claims – A Practical Guide for the Personal Injury Practitioner' by Greg Almond
'Intercompany Agreements for Transfer Pricing Compliance' by Paul Sutton
'Zen and the Art of Mediation' by Martin Plowman
'A Practical Guide to the SRA Principles, Individual and Law Firm Codes of Conduct 2019 – What Every Law Firm Needs to Know' by Paul Bennett
'A Practical Guide to Adoption for Family Lawyers' by Graham Pegg
'A Practical Guide to Industrial Disease Claims' by Andrew Mckie & Ian Skeate
'A Practical Guide to Redundancy' by Philip Hyland
'A Practical Guide to Vicarious Liability' by Mariel Irvine
'A Practical Guide to Applications for Landlord's Consent and Variation of Leases' by Mark Shelton
'A Practical Guide to Relief from Sanctions Post-Mitchell and Denton' by Peter Causton
'A Practical Guide to Equity Release for Advisors' by Paul Sams
'A Practical Guide to the Law Relating to Food' by Ian Thomas
'A Practical Guide to Financial Services Claims' by Chris Hegarty
'The Law of Houses in Multiple Occupation: A Practical Guide to HMO Proceedings' by Julian Hunt
'A Practical Guide to Unlawful Eviction and Harassment' by Stephanie Lovegrove
'Occupiers, Highways and Defective Premises Claims: A Practical Guide Post-Jackson – 2nd Edition' by Andrew Mckie

'A Practical Guide to Financial Ombudsman Service Claims' by Adam Temple & Robert Scrivenor
'A Practical Guide to Advising Schools on Employment Law' by Jonathan Holden
'A Practical Guide to Running Housing Disrepair and Cavity Wall Claims: 2nd Edition' by Andrew Mckie & Ian Skeate
'A Practical Guide to Holiday Sickness Claims – 2nd Edition' by Andrew Mckie & Ian Skeate
'Arguments and Tactics for Personal Injury and Clinical Negligence Claims' by Dorian Williams
'A Practical Guide to Drone Law' by Rufus Ballaster, Andrew Firman, Eleanor Clot
'A Practical Guide to Compliance for Personal Injury Firms Working With Claims Management Companies' by Paul Bennett
'A Practical Guide to Dog Law for Owners and Others' by Andrea Pitt
'RTA Allegations of Fraud in a Post-Jackson Era: The Handbook – 2nd Edition' by Andrew Mckie
'RTA Personal Injury Claims: A Practical Guide Post-Jackson' by Andrew Mckie
'On Experts: CPR35 for Lawyers and Experts' by David Boyle
'An Introduction to Personal Injury Law' by David Boyle
'A Practical Guide to Subtle Brain Injury Claims' by Pankaj Madan

These books and more are available to order online direct from the publisher at www.lawbriefpublishing.com, where you can also read free sample chapters. For any queries, contact us on 0844 587 2383 or mail@lawbriefpublishing.com.

Our books are also usually in stock at www.amazon.co.uk with free next day delivery for Prime members, and at good legal bookshops such as Wildy & Sons.

We are regularly launching new books in our series of practical day-to-day practitioners' guides. Visit our website and join our free newsletter to be kept informed and to receive special offers, free chapters, etc.

You can also follow us on Twitter at www.twitter.com/lawbriefpub.

www.ingramcontent.com/pod-product-compliance
Ingram Content Group UK Ltd.
Pitfield, Milton Keynes, MK11 3LW, UK
UKHW020149290926
15471UKWH00004B/777

9 781913 715298